A Bible Study by

Melissa Spoelstra

First Corinthians

Living Love
When We Disagree

Abingdon Women / Nashville

First Corinthians
Living Love When We Disagree

This book is printed on elemental chlorine-free paper.

ISBN 978-1-5018-0168-6

19 20 21 22 23 24 25 — 10 9 8
MANUFACTURED IN THE UNITED STATES OF AMERICA

CONTENTS

ABOUT THE AUTHOR

Melissa Spoelstra is a popular women's conference speaker, Bible teacher, and author who is madly in love with Jesus and passionate about studying God's Word and helping women of all ages to seek Christ and know Him more intimately through serious Bible study. Having a degree in Bible theology, she enjoys teaching God's Word to the body of Christ, traveling to diverse groups and churches across the nation and also to Nairobi, Kenya, for a women's prayer conference. Melissa is the author of the Bible studies *Joseph: The Journey to Forgiveness* and *Jeremiah: Daring to Hope in an Unstable World* and the parenting book *Total Family Makeover: 8 Practical Steps to Making Disciples at Home.* She has published articles in *ParentLife, Women's Spectrum, Just Between Us,* and the Women of Faith blog. She also writes her own regular blog in which she shares her musings about what God is teaching her on any given day. Melissa lives in Dublin, Ohio, with her pastor husband, Sean, and their four kids: Zach, Abby, Sara, and Rachel.

Follow Melissa:

Twitter	@MelSpoelstra
Instagram	@Daring2Hope
Facebook	@AuthorMelissaSpoelstra
Her blog	MelissaSpoelstra.com (check here also for event dates and booking information)

Introduction

Living love when we disagree sounds good on paper, but it isn't easy. We're different—we have different personalities, preferences, and perspectives. And we can struggle to get along, especially when we don't see eye to eye. In the course of a day, we can find ourselves disagreeing or debating with family, friends, coworkers, and even strangers on social media about everything from food choices and parenting styles to politics and religion. Often we find ourselves divided—even as Christians. How can we work out our differences with humility and grace, always showing the love of Christ, while still remaining true to what we believe?

The Apostle Paul wrote a letter to the church in Corinth about this very thing, because they were struggling with their own set of issues. Being one of the few churches where both Jews and Gentiles worshiped together, they had different practices and ideas that threatened unity in the church. Their economic and social diversity contributed to the discord, giving them a reputation for conflict. Rather than focusing on Christ as the head of the body, they formed factions based on various church leaders. Worship practices, the role of women, and sensitive issues of conscience were other topics of concern. Paul addressed all of these divisive issues in his letter, which we know today as 1 Corinthians.

Paul urged the church in Corinth to "be of one mind, united in thought and purpose" (1 Corinthians 1:10). He essentially called them to live love—even when they disagreed. Chapter 13, known as the love chapter, wasn't included to be a nice poem for weddings. Instead, it was written to urge Christians living in a pagan and diverse culture to approach one another with the love of Christ. It calls us to do the same.

Regrettably, we often exercise the opposite of that kind of love, choosing instead to keep a record of wrongs or to make rude comments—whether in person or on social media. The truth is, we can never demonstrate this supernatural love and kindness with those who disagree with us apart from Jesus. Paul acknowledged this truth, mentioning the name of Jesus nine times in the first nine verses of this letter alone! He knew that we desperately need Christ at the center of our personal lives, including our interactions with others. Our unity comes only through Christ and His love.

In the next six weeks, we will dive deep into Paul's letter, exploring how we can:

- Deal with our differences in a loving way without compromising our convictions
- Achieve harmony while maintaining our diversity
- Consider the ways that the surrounding culture impacts our beliefs
- Agree to disagree on matters of preference and opinion
- Humbly listen to others with views different than our own
- Embrace ambiguity in some areas, acknowledging that our view is often partial and incomplete
- Demonstrate to all that love is the greatest thing, which never fails

Together we will learn some practical truths we can implement in our relationships in order to live love even when we disagree. We will see that Paul's call to unity isn't a call to compromise our beliefs. Just as he upheld the gospel of Christ while seeking to help the Corinthians apply it to their relationships, we too will discover how we can stand firm on the gospel while finding and focusing on our common ground in Christ.

Options for Study

Before beginning the study, I invite you to consider the level of commitment your time and life circumstances will allow. I have found that what I put into a Bible study directly correlates to what I get out of it. When I take time to do the homework daily, God's truths sink deeper as I take time to reflect and meditate on what God is teaching me. When I am intentional about gathering with other women to watch videos and have discussion, I find that this helps keep me from falling off the Bible study wagon midway. Also, making a point to memorize verses and dig deeper by looking at additional materials greatly benefits my soul.

At other times, however, I have bitten off more than I can chew. When our faith is new, our children are small, or there are great demands on our time because of difficult circumstances or challenges, we need to be realistic about what we will be able to finish. So this study is designed with options that enable you to tailor it for your particular circumstances and needs.

1. Basic Study. The basic study includes five daily readings or lessons. Each lesson combines study of Scripture with personal reflection and application (**green boldface type** indicates write-in-the-book questions and activities), ending with a suggestion for talking with God about what you've learned. On average you will need about twenty to thirty minutes to complete each lesson.

When you gather with your group to review each week's material, you will watch a video, discuss what you are learning, and pray together. I encourage you to discuss the insights you are gaining and how God is working in your own life.

2. Deeper Study. If you want an even deeper study, there is a Weekly Wrap-up at the end of each week to guide you in reviewing the chapters and themes covered that week. This will give you a better sense of the flow of the letter, which was designed to be read out loud and passed among the house churches in Corinth. Additionally, Digging Deeper articles are available online (see www.AbingdonPress.com/FirstCorinthians) for those who would like deeper exploration of the text and themes. Finally, memory verses are provided for each week of study so that you may meditate on and memorize key truths from God's Word.

3. Lighter Commitment. If you are in a season of life in which you need a lighter commitment, I encourage you to give yourself permission to do what you can. God will bless your efforts and speak to you through this study at every level of participation.

Take time now to pray and decide which level of study is right for you, and check it below:

__ **1. Basic Study**

__ **2. Deeper Study**

__ **3. Lighter Commitment**

Be sure to let someone in your group know which level of study you plan to do so that you have some accountability and encouragement.

Also, I invite you to post some of the insights and experiences you and your group have during the study, using the hashtag #1Corinthians. If a verse or sentence from the study stands out to you, feel free to tweet, Instagram, or Facebook using the hashtag so that we can see what is resonating with you!

A Final Word

As we begin this journey together, keep in mind that the goal is unity in Christ, not uniformity. The body of Christ is made up of unique individuals with different gifts, opinions, and ideologies; and there is strength and beauty in that diversity. Although achieving harmony in the midst of our diversity may be challenging, it is not impossible. God never calls us to do something without equipping us through His Word and His Spirit. With the help of the Spirit of Christ who lives within us, we can learn to deal with our differences in a loving way—even while living in a divided culture. May this powerful truth from 1 Corinthians 13:8 (NIV) both encourage and motivate us: *Love never fails!*

Week 1

IN CHRIST ALONE

1 Corinthians 1–2

Memory Verse

I appeal to you, dear brothers and sisters, by the authority of our Lord Jesus Christ, to live in harmony with each other. Let there be no divisions in the church. Rather, be of one mind, united in thought and purpose.

(1 Corinthians 1:10)

DAY 1: SPIRITUAL IDENTITY

My pastor husband, Sean, and I host a gathering on the second Sunday of every month. We invite new people who have visited our church so they can ask questions and we can share a little about the church's vision and values. It's an informal time when we try to keep it real by mentioning our weaknesses and past mistakes as a church as well as the exciting things God is doing in our midst.

Imagine you are a visitor checking out the church in Corinth. Here are some of the things you might discover by asking questions at a gathering in the home of a church leader:

- People are identifying with certain preferred leaders and teachers to the extent that factions exist within the local body.
- Members are divided over whether the man in the church who is having an affair with his stepmother is exercising newfound freedom from the law or is in need of church discipline.
- Believers are bringing lawsuits against each other.
- There are differing opinions about marriage, men's and women's roles in the church, and abuses of spiritual gifts.

While we might decide to visit the church down the street, the early believers had no such option. They had to learn to work out their differences.

Whether or not they are apparent to everyone, all churches struggle with divisions and difficulties. The church is not only *made up* of sinners but also is *led* by sinners. Until we reach heaven, no perfect body of believers will exist. And sometimes we fight over some of the silliest things!

The Corinthian church had its issues for sure, but our church situations aren't much different. Are there those in your church who are constantly quoting some popular preacher they are enamored with? What about people who disagree about which sins the church should address and which should be left to an individual's conviction of the Holy Spirit? Have disputes ever arisen after two believers saw a business deal fall apart or had different opinions about how a ministry should be run? Though we may not like to admit it, our churches can be just as dysfunctional as the Corinthian body of believers.

Extra Insight

Corinth was located on an isthmus between two seas, which gave it importance as a commercial center as well as a strategic military position.

What are some disagreements you've observed in the Christian community of which you are a part?

Some members of the pilot group for this study mentioned disagreements about:

- contemporary worship
- whether to have a choir
- the layout of the church bulletin
- whether the American flag should be on display in the sanctuary
- what the Bible says about salvation, marriage, and other topics

The question isn't whether we will have disagreements in the church but how we will handle these conflicts.

When the local leaders in Corinth weren't sure how to handle some of these conflicts, they wrote a letter to the man who had founded the church. Paul had helped to plant the church while on his second missionary journey when he stayed in Corinth for a year and a half. He began preaching in the Jewish synagogue but ended up gathering more converts from a Gentile audience. Believers came from all socioeconomic classes and included a minority of Jewish converts. While they were united in Christ, their diversity caused many disagreements.

Though we do not have a copy of the original letter, the Book of First Corinthians contains the Apostle Paul's response to questions written about three to five years after the birth of the church. At this time Paul was ministering in the city of Ephesus while attempting to instruct and encourage the believers in Corinth through his writings. Understanding the context of the letter as well as the backdrop of Corinthian culture will help us make sense of those portions that can be difficult for us to understand today. Despite our cultural differences, the issues the early Corinthian believers faced have continued to cause debate and conflict in the church for two thousand years, resulting in disagreements on subjects such as men's and women's roles and the practice of spiritual gifts.

As we study Paul's letter, we'll find a call to quit majoring in the minors. This reminds me of the motto of the Moravian Church, whose roots date back to the fifteenth century: "In essentials, unity; in nonessentials, liberty; and in all things, love."[1] God used Paul as His mouthpiece to help the early church learn to love each other and work toward unity. Sometimes love meant confronting blatant sin, and other times it meant backing down on preference issues that weren't black or white. As we go through a section of the letter each day, we'll be looking for the original meaning as well as the contemporary significance.

Before we get into the text, let's consider a few facts about the city of Corinth:

- Corinth had been a prominent port city that the Romans destroyed in 146 B.C., and it rose again to prominence when Julius Caesar rebuilt the city in 44 B.C.
- At the time of Paul's writing (A.D. 55), the city was about one hundred years old and had a population of around 80,000 with another 20,000 in outlying areas.
- Corinth was a wealthy and multicultural city.
- A major attraction in Corinth was a temple to Aphrodite (the Greek goddess of love) that boasted 1,000 temple prostitutes.
- The Corinthians held strongly the Greek ideals of individualism, equality, freedom, and distrust of authority.[2]

In a nutshell, the rebuilt city of Corinth was a melting pot of cultures with new wealth and an emphasis on intelligence and individualism.

What modern cities come to mind when you read about Corinth?

What parallels do you find between Corinthian culture and our culture?

Did you think of cities known for their wealth, sin, or proximity to bodies of water? I believe we will find many ways to relate to the believers in Corinth though we are separated by almost two thousand years.

Before Paul addressed any of the Corinthians' questions, he settled the issue of identity. Over and over he repeated the name of Christ.

Read 1 Corinthians 1:1-9, holding your place here for today's study. How many times did Paul mention Christ's name?

Paul began his letter with an emphasis on his personal relationship to Christ and reminded the Corinthians that their source of grace and peace was found in Christ. Two times Paul mentioned the return of Christ to give them an eternal perspective in the midst of their disagreements. Anyone reading just these first nine verses can't help knowing Paul's favorite topic of conversation.

Paul would go on to offer admonishments, instructions, and truths that might be tough to swallow, but he began with encouragement about Christ—knowing that Christ should be the starting point for every discussion and disagreement. Apart from Him we are just blowing smoke with shared ignorance.

Next Paul reminded the Corinthians that God made them holy. The word used here means set apart or different. Then he said that not only the Corinthian believers were holy through Christ, but others were as well.

Who, specifically, did Paul say are holy in verse 2?

If all who call on the name of Christ are made holy, what does that mean you are?

If you have called on the name of Christ for salvation, then you have been made holy. So many times that is not how I see myself. I feel lazy when I don't get everything done on my to-do list. Discouragement can overtake me for no good reason at all. Sometimes I look to people or possessions for validation. On any given day I can be tempted to find my identity in anything from my pants size to my children's behavior. These last few days I've been in a funk, and I'm not really sure why. Rather than celebrate the wonderful things going on in life, I want to crawl under the covers and stay there. I don't feel holy. Yet Christ says that I am.

So the question for me and you is *which posture will we claim today?* Will we find our identity in

- how we feel,
- what we've accomplished,
- our appearance,
- how others view us,
- or what Christ says about us?

Paul wanted so intensely for the Corinthians to remember their holy identity that he mentioned Christ's name repeatedly. He made it clear that they were set apart and special not because of their wealth, talents, or feelings but because of Christ's death on the cross.

No grades of holiness exist. Some people aren't "kind of holy" and others are "super holy." If you are a believer, then you are holy through the blood of Christ—period. Holiness isn't something we attain. Christ imputed it to us through His sacrifice on the cross. Before we embark any further into a controversial letter with topics that threaten to divide us as believers, let's settle the issue of our shared identity.

While we may disagree on many things within the Christian community, the lens we should view one another through is holiness. We and our brothers and sisters in Christ are holy because Jesus Christ set us apart through His shed blood. He paid the highest price so that we could be called holy. Consider what impact that embracing this identity could have on our words, actions, and prayers toward those with whom we are struggling to get along.

Consider the disagreements you have observed within the body of Christ. How could seeing ourselves and one another as holy help with conflict resolution? (Answers will vary; there is no one right answer.)

Paul began his letter to the church at Corinth with a greeting and an emphasis on our shared identity in Christ to set the tone for the sixteen chapters of admonition and encouragement that followed. He also stressed his authority as an apostle because, as we will see, many in the church were rejecting his leadership. How could Paul be so positive about a church full of divisions? He could have let their struggles become a reason to write them off and focus on other churches he had planted that didn't seem as problematic. Instead, he turned his attention to the character of God. He recognized what one commentator has so beautifully expressed: "To delight in God for his working in the lives of others, even in the lives of those with whom one feels compelled to disagree, is sure evidence of one's own awareness of being the recipient of God's mercies."[3]

A common tendency among many Christians today is to find a new faith community when the human flaws of their church are exposed. As we study 1 Corinthians, I pray we will see other believers for who they really are—struggling sinners like us whom Christ has declared holy. Then we will be able to celebrate one another's strengths before beginning to work out our disagreements.

Talk with God

In the blank below, write the name or first initial of a believer you have disagreed with recently—even if only in your thoughts.

_____ is holy and loved by God through Christ.

Take a moment to pray for this person, asking God to help you see him or her as God does.

Extra Insight

The very last verse in the Bible reminds us that we can view one another as holy. As the final words of God's revelation to us, John wrote, "May the grace of the Lord Jesus be with God's holy people" (Revelation 22:21).

As a follower of Christ, write your name in the blank below:

_____ is accepted by God and declared holy because she has called on the name of the Lord Jesus Christ. "But to all who believed him and accepted him, he gave the right to become children of God" (John 1:12).

Write a prayer in the margin thanking God that your identity is not based on your accomplishments, feelings, clothing size, or number of likes on social media. Also thank Him for the cross and your holiness found in Christ alone.

DAY 2: DEALING WITH DIVISIONS

Of course, there are going to be times when we disagree with one another as Christians. However, the manner in which we disagree gives the watching world a glimpse of how followers of Jesus are interacting, and often it's not a good picture—especially when our viewpoints don't align on anything from the exposed sins of a prominent Christian leader to our interpretations of a particular passage of Scripture.

Online I read hateful words, witness name calling, and watch Scripture bullies use God's Word as a weapon against fellow believers. The Bible is a sword, but we are called to wield it against our common enemy, Satan, not each other. Through this letter to the church in Corinth, Paul models the need to address conflicts with the recipe for healing divisions among us. Whether we are sparring online, via text, over the phone, or face to face, Paul teaches us that God asks us to strive for unity, especially in the midst of our disagreements.

We don't have to conform and be cookie cutter Christians who agree on every minute point of doctrine. Of course, theology matters. Paul wasn't propagating an "anything goes" attitude toward the Scriptures. On the contrary, his letter sought to help realign the Corinthians in areas where they strayed from sound teaching, resulting in divisions. The key to finding resolution is in separating preferences from absolutes. Many times we squabble over minutia and miss the big picture.

Today we're going to look at two specific dangers Paul addressed that can lead to divisions.

1. Relational Idolatry

The first danger Paul addressed is relational idolatry. Anything that captures our attention more than God can become an idol, including people. And often the result is divisive allegiances.

Read 1 Corinthians 1:10-17 and rewrite verse 10 in your own words, inserting the name of your church:

What did Paul say was the source of the quarrels between the people in the church at Corinth? (v. 12)

How did Paul hear about the quarrels? (v. 11)

Extra Insight

Most of Paul's letters begin with doctrinal truth followed by a section of practical application, but in 1 Corinthians Paul "plunges immediately into the problems of the church."[5]

In this instance, *divisions* is translated from the Greek word *schism*, which was a political term for "rival parties or factions."[4] Like members of a political party fiercely supporting their candidate, the Corinthians rallied around a particular Christian leader. As we bridge the gap between the church at Corinth and our local bodies of believers today, we recognize that we too struggle with making celebrities out of Christian leaders.

When I was in high school I witnessed a group of people in our church who were mesmerized with a particular leader, resulting in what almost seemed like a cult following. They quoted him often, went to his conferences, purchased his workbooks, and embraced his particular ideas about following Jesus, which emphasized things such as clothing and appearance. I remember wondering why things that had no biblical support had become so important.

In what ways have you seen people seem overly enamored with Christian personalities and their teachings?

Because Paul had to be told about the quarrels, he probably had not contributed to the rivaling groups. Many times the people we venerate after hearing them teach, reading their books, or following their blogs desire only to point us to Christ. Yet we like to attach ourselves to human leaders much as the people in the church of Corinth did. Instead, God calls us through Paul's letter to seek unity.

Paul called the Corinthians to be of the same mind or thought (v. 10). The Greek word he used is *nous*, which is defined as "the mind, comprising alike the faculties of perceiving and understanding and those of feeling, judging, determining."[6] Paul used an additional word to emphasize that

God wants us to be perfectly united not only in our minds but also in our purpose or judgment. This Greek word is *gnome,* meaning "the faculty of knowledge, mind, reason."[7]

Judgment has become a negative word today, but let's remember that God wants us to exercise good judgment. He longs for us to evaluate conversations, statements, actions, and relationships with unity at the forefront. This certainly doesn't mean checking our brains at the door, but it does mean using our God-given sense to see the harm in getting too attached to a particular human leader.

In verse 12, Paul identifies some of the leaders the Corinthians were elevating. List them below:

1.

2.

3.

4.

Paul listed himself first. People were drawn to him as the founder of the Corinthian church. He was like a spiritual father to many, having been the one who first preached the gospel to many of the members.

The second leader was Apollos.

Read Acts 18:24-26. Why do you believe some Corinthian believers would have been drawn to Apollos?

Apollos taught eloquently, enthusiastically, and with accuracy. His knowledge of the Scriptures and smooth style would have appealed to educated people as well as those with a desire for in-depth teaching.

The third leader Paul mentioned is Peter. Peter knew Jesus personally when He walked the earth. Peter's boldness, miracles, and authority on the day of Pentecost would have caused many to be in awe of him. (Can you imagine them bragging, "After all, he *did* walk on water!")

The last group claimed to follow only Christ. At first this Sunday school answer—"I follow Jesus"—seems like it couldn't be wrong. However, most commentators agree that Paul was lumping together those who were righteous with those who were smug. The attitude of the latter almost seemed to say, "We are of Christ, but we aren't so sure about *you.*"

We can see people venerating these same types of leaders today—the spiritual father or shepherd (Paul), the academic teacher (Apollos), and the bold, authoritative leader (Peter). Others are like those in the last group, who won't look to any human authority—other than themselves. Yet whenever a Christian leader's charisma or celebrity overshadows the cross of Christ, danger lies ahead.

As followers of Jesus, 1 Thessalonians 5:12 calls us to respect our leaders. Some things Scripture admonishes us to do in regard to leaders are to

- provide for their needs (1 Timothy 5:17),
- imitate their faith (Hebrews 13:7),
- obey them without complaining (Hebrews 13:17),
- pray for them (1 Timothy 2:1),
- and share good things with them (Galatians 6:6).

Though God calls us to honor our leaders, we must not idolize them. They are humans who sin just as we do. We must be careful not to magnify the messenger and miss the message.

I have been guilty of listening to a message and being more enamored with the speaking style, illustrations, or delivery than with personally applying the truths presented. My thoughts can turn to grading the speaker rather than asking the Holy Spirit to convict and encourage me. Can you relate?

What are some ways you have been tempted to overly identify with one or more Christian leaders?

We all have heroes in the faith, and this is not a bad thing. We just need to be cautious not to get out of balance. Like a pendulum, we can swing too far to one side and elevate a person to larger-than-life status, making us "sheeple" who follow without question. Or we can swing too far to the other side and demonstrate our refusal to show respect for those with God-given authority, becoming critical skeptics. I've been at women's conferences where a certain teacher actually needed bodyguards because of stalking "sheeples" who demanded attention. On the flip side, I recently received an e-mail through my website from a skeptic who questioned one of my video teachings after misunderstanding the heart of the message. Rather than swinging too far in either direction, the key is to stay balanced in the center.

Take a few moments now to pray, asking God if you are out of balance in relation to any Christian leaders, teachers (including authors and speakers), preachers, or musicians. Consider those you are *drawn to*—in the church, on the radio or television, at conferences or concerts, or on social media—as well as those you are *not* drawn to and may find yourself openly criticizing.

> We must be careful not to magnify the messenger and miss the message.

Read the following descriptions. Below Skeptic, list any Christian leaders you may be highly critical of. Below Sheeple, list any you may tend to put on a pedestal. Finally, inside the pendulum write the names of a few leaders you follow with a balanced approach. Include one of your local Christian leaders in this category.

Skeptic
General distrustful feeling toward them
Wouldn't receive correction well from them
Criticize them to others often
Usually disagree with decisions they make

Sheeple
Quote them often
Read them more than Bible
Rarely question what they say
Mildly obsessed with their ministry

Balanced Approach
You benefit from their God-given gifts
Want to imitate their faith
Draw closer to Jesus through their ministry
You check their words against Scripture when something doesn't sound right
You can agree to disagree with them on certain points since no one person has all truth

Which tendency do you identify with more—skeptic or sheeple?

Extra Insight

Urban dictionary defines *sheeple* as "people unable to think for themselves. Followers. Lemmings. Those with no cognitive abilities of their own."[8]

Some Corinthian believers swung to the sheeple side regarding Apollos or Peter, which caused them to swing to the skeptic side concerning Paul's authority. Both of these extremes lead to factions and divisions. God wants us to have a balanced approach toward our leaders. We are to learn from them and honor them, but we also must realize they have feet of clay and sometimes get it wrong. I tend to question everything and find myself with skeptic leanings. But once I've developed an affinity for a certain Bible teacher, my pendulum tends to swing to the other side where it seems he or she can do or say nothing wrong. I'm learning to find balance.

Write a short prayer below, asking God to help you restore balance in any areas where the messenger may have become magnified above the message in your Christian walk:

2. Outward Signs of Inward Changes

The second danger Paul mentioned has to do with arguments over outward signs of inward changes.

Some Corinthian believers sought status based on who baptized them. Though we may not argue about that specifically, church history reveals a lot of schism over the baptismal waters. Some of the greatest theologians in history such as Zwingli, Calvin, Luther, and Wesley argued vehemently for what they deemed the correct methods of participating in baptism and communion. Regardless of our practices and terminology related to baptism and Communion, we must remember that they are a gift from God, not another brand of strife for the church.

On the night before his crucifixion, Jesus prayed these words:

> [20]*"My prayer is not for them alone. I pray also for those who will believe in me through their message,* [21] *that all of them may be one, Father, just as you are in me and I am in you. May they also be in us so that the world may believe that you have sent me.* [22] *I have given them the glory that you gave me, that they may be one as we are one—* [23] *I in them and you in me—so that they may be brought to complete unity. Then the world will know that you sent me and have loved them even as you have loved me."*
>
> *(John 17:20-23 NIV)*

Jesus' prayer was for us. He knows our propensity toward division and the twisting of beautiful expressions of faith into dividing lines. He prayed for us because He understands our weaknesses. Jesus longs for us to have complete unity, and I believe this includes the outward manifestations of inward changes that He instituted during His earthly ministry. While we may disagree about how we practice these observances, we should be unified in the heart behind them, remembering that they point to Christ. Yet often we argue over the very things that Jesus gave us as tangible reminders of His love and sacrifice. We must guard against elevating form over substance.

In His prayer, Jesus said that our unity would showcase Him to the world. When we fight over outward expressions of our faith—such as our preference of worship music, preaching styles, church décor, methods of baptism, modes of Communion, or anything else on the long list of things we squabble about—we don't draw unbelievers to the incredible truth and power of the cross. As one commentator has noted, "Church should be a place where people who have no other natural reason for associating with each other come together in love, but instead it often remains the most segregated aspect of Western society today."[9]

How have you seen unity expressed among believers in the midst of differing opinions?

Some examples of this kind of unity might include a Bible study group that includes women from different denominations or a collaboration of believers who disagree on many issues coming together to serve the community. While there are no simple answers to healing fractures among the body of Christ, we can strive to achieve unity without uniformity. Paul didn't appeal to the Corinthians to stop the factions among them based on expediency or tolerance. Instead, he tried to persuade them to be unified based on one reason.

Christ didn't send me to baptize, but to preach the Good News—and not with clever speech, for fear that the cross of Christ would lose its power. (1 Corinthians 1:17)

According to 1 Corinthians 1:17 (in the margin), what did Paul say Christ sent him to do?

Paul wasn't saying baptism has no value; instead he claimed that all other things recede into the background in light of the cross of Christ. One scholar puts it this way: "Paul says that cliquishness in the church serves to chop Christ up in pieces and parcel Him out. When we identify ourselves only with this piece or that portion of Jesus, we lose our perspective on the whole of Christian theology."[10]

When we reflect on the cross and the anguish, sweat, and blood of Christ; the loneliness and pain He experienced when the Father turned His face away; the weight of sin; and Christ's death and resurrection—all on our behalf—all other disagreements take a backseat. The cross wasn't a cute logo the early church came up with to solidify their brand. It was an instrument of torture. Like featuring an electric chair or lethal injection on your website, the cross was an unlikely marketing magnet to draw people to salvation. Yet it was God's perfect plan for atonement. The cross exposes our sins of pride, hatred, and disunity with others. Through the shed blood of Christ we find healing—for ourselves and our fractured relationships in the church.

Typically when I have argued over outward expressions of faith to the point that it causes division, I usually find pride and self-righteousness creeping into my soul. The cross helps us remember who we really are: sinners desperately in need of a Savior trying to get along with other sinners desperately in need of a Savior.

Paul wasn't advocating that the Corinthians throw out all sound doctrine and teaching other than the gospel message itself. As we progress through his letter, we will find him very clearly confronting all sorts of doctrinal issues. He simply wanted to be sure that they approached differences from the perspective of the cross. We are called to do the same. Then, with an attitude of humility and grace, we can discuss our varied viewpoints without creating factions and divisions within the body of Christ. The cross helps us reimagine who we really are, aligning in unity all who follow Jesus.

Talk with God

Take a moment to reread 1 Corinthians 1:10-17. Then rewrite in your own words the two dangers we identified in today's study that can lead to division:

1.

2.

Now write Paul's primary focus according to verse 17:

Spend some time in prayer, meditating on what Jesus did on the cross. Thank Him for how He has cleansed you, changed you, and healed you. Then ask Him to help you, as well as your church, dissipate all petty disagreements and complicated divisions through the healing power of the cross.

DAY 3: THE FOOLISH PLAN OF GOD

When my family moved into our first house over sixteen years ago, we quickly discovered that our neighbors had a little girl similar in age to our two-year-old son. Our toddlers became fast friends and played together for years until the whole "I'm a boy and it's not cool to play with girls" thing took effect. This gal's mom and I enjoyed a sweet friendship as we celebrated kids' birthdays, took walks, and encouraged each other through two more pregnancies for each of us. While this family respected our faith, they didn't share it. One summer we had a backyard Bible club in our garage, and their daughter, who I'll call Jennifer, came every day. She was about nine years old at the time. When the stories were told, Jennifer listened intently. On the last day I shared the simple gospel message, and she indicated that she wanted to have a personal relationship with Jesus.

The next day I called her mom, holding the phone in my trembling hands. I didn't want my friend to think we were brainwashing her daughter. I nervously asked if we could meet for lunch. After the small

Extra Insight

The church at Corinth likely was made up of multiple house churches meeting in different parts of town. "The seeds of rivalry could have been sown by those geographical divisions as well."[11]

talk about kids and husbands ended, I began to tell her about Jennifer's decision to become a Christ-follower. She inquired what exactly I meant by that statement. I shared with her the basic lesson that had prompted Jennifer to respond:

- God's great love for us. (John 3:16)
- Our sin separates us from this Holy God. (Romans 3:23)
- Christ died on the cross as the payment for our sin to reunite us with God. (Romans 4:25 and 5:8)
- When we personally receive Christ as our Lord and Savior we become children of God who receive eternal life. (John 1:12, Romans 10:9)

I told her that Jennifer said she believed those truths and wanted to have a personal relationship with God through Christ. As I was talking, I could tell that she was really listening and thinking. She said something like this: "Are you are saying that if I live a good, moral life trying to make the best decisions I can and love my family but never admit that I'm a sinner and ask Christ into my life, then I will not go to heaven? But if a rapist or murderer in jail believes these truths and asks God to forgive him through Christ, then he will go to heaven? That makes no sense to me." She had never heard the truths of the gospel that I shared, and she had trouble wrapping her mind around God's plan of salvation.

How would you explain God's plan of salvation to a nonbelieving friend?

Today as we read 1 Corinthians 1:18-31, we will hear Paul reiterating the truth that the intersection of God's plan and what seems logical to us often creates some cognitive dissonance. We will see that he emphasized three key themes that can help us wrap our minds around God's sovereign plans, which often surpass human wisdom:

1. The Message of the Cross
2. The Futility of Human Wisdom
3. Boasting with Humility

1. The Message of the Cross

The first theme we encounter in this section of Paul's letter is the message of the cross. The cross is central to the gospel and God's plan of salvation, yet it can be a cause for confusion and division—even among Christians.

Read 1 Corinthians 1:18-25. What are the two outcomes for the two different views about the cross according to verse 18?

View   Outcome

Message of the cross is foolish   _____

Message of the cross is the power of God   _____

Is there a third position, or does everyone fall into one of these two camps?

Read Luke 11:23 in the margin. How do these words of Jesus support or weaken your conclusion?

Now read Romans 1:16 in the margin. How does this verse support 1 Corinthians 1:18?

We find no fence-sitting when it comes to our belief about Christ. Paul delved into the message of the cross because unity is quickly threatened when it's not at the center of our lives.

I'm happy to tell you that when Jennifer's family was about to move out of town, I shared with her mother a little book written by Andy Stanley called *Since Nobody's Perfect: How Good Is Good Enough?* It basically takes the "good people go to heaven" theory that so many people espouse and explains in a clear, concise way why it has a lack of biblical support. I wasn't sure my friend would read it, but she called a few days later and mentioned that she had read the whole thing and felt that she finally "got it." Now it made sense: good people don't go to heaven; forgiven people do. And she too responded to God's invitation of grace.

Paul was reminding the believers at Corinth that the message of the cross must be central to all of life and practice, but it is especially crucial in regards to how we view ourselves and others. We can't count on religiosity, rules, or human wisdom to help us live love when we disagree. Without the message of the cross, all of those things are useless.

"Anyone who isn't with me opposes me, and anyone who isn't working with me is actually working against me."
(Luke 11:23)

I am not ashamed of this Good News about Christ. It is the power of God at work, saving everyone who believes—the Jew first and also the Gentile.
(Romans 1:16)

When did you make a personal decision to follow Christ? Or if you've loved Jesus since you were a very young child, when did you begin to understand the message of the cross?

How might your life be different if the message of the cross was foolish to you? What might you have done differently regarding certain decisions, attitudes, and relationships?

2. The Futility of Human Wisdom

After focusing on the message of the cross, Paul went on to reference a verse from the prophet Isaiah about God destroying wisdom and intelligence. This idea can be confusing to us rational human beings. Here is what God *isn't* saying: "Leave your brain at the door. There is little value in thinking, investigating, asking questions, furthering your education, dialoguing about concepts, or studying." This portion of Paul's letter is not an out for thinking deeply, asking questions, or taking the time to read and study. In fact, it is through study and investigation that we find context in Paul's reference to Isaiah's words.

As the Scriptures say,

"I will destroy the wisdom of the wise and discard the intelligence of the intelligent."
(1 Corinthians 1:19)

Read 1 Corinthians 1:19 in the margin. Then read the verses from Isaiah below, underlining the portion that Paul references in 1 Corinthians 1:19.

¹³ *And so the Lord says,*

  "These people say they are mine.

They honor me with their lips,

  but their hearts are far from me.

And their worship of me

  is nothing but man-made rules learned by rote.

¹⁴ *Because of this, I will once again astound these hypocrites*

  with amazing wonders.

The wisdom of the wise will pass away,

  and the intelligence of the intelligent will disappear."

(Isaiah 29:13-14)

From the prophet Isaiah we learn that God rejects lip service and rules followed by rote but favors authenticity and brokenness over the pretense of human righteousness (see Isaiah 29:13). God isn't calling us to blissful ignorance but is reminding us that His way is always best. God also used the prophet Isaiah to speak this important message: "For just as the heavens are higher than the earth, / so my ways are higher than your ways / and my thoughts higher than your thoughts" (55:9). In other words, what sounds like the most logical plan to us might not be best.

From the perspective of hindsight, when and how have God's plans worked out better than your own plans?

Paul was reminding the Corinthians that the God of Isaiah was still the same God—and He is the same God today. His ways are still much better than ours. Only He knows what is best for us in every situation. Sometimes I exhaust my own ways trying to fix my problems with strategy, logic, and even manipulation before asking God for His wisdom in a situation. Often He asks us to do something that doesn't make sense, such as:

- Be still in the midst of a battle raging around us. (Moses, Exodus 14)
- Trust Him even when a problem seems hopeless. (Hezekiah, 2 Kings 19)
- Speak bold messages of hope even when no one is listening. (Jeremiah, Jeremiah 7:26-27)

What can you add to this list? When has God's wisdom not been in alignment with what made sense or felt right to you?

The Corinthians lived in a culture where intellect was overemphasized. One authority writes, "Corinth paid special attention to people who could speak well, public rhetoricians, lawyers and the like. The wise, the powerful, the noble: these were the 'somebodies' in Corinth."[12] Paul wasn't advocating an abandonment of the pursuit of wisdom. Rather, he was reminding the Corinthians that relying solely on our often skewed human faculties will bring faulty conclusions. We find truth when we humbly recognize that God is the only reliable source of wisdom. This passage isn't anti-thinking; Paul was realigning the Corinthian believers to the superior nature of God's wisdom, which makes human logic and wisdom look foolish in comparison. Because the Corinthian culture was bent toward human wisdom, it was necessary to acknowledge and emphasize the truth of the "foolishness" of the cross.

If Paul had been writing to another church where education wasn't valued, he might have pressed them to study more. Having children with different learning styles, I understand this. I might go into one of my daughter's rooms and talk to her about the need to work harder at her schoolwork and get assignments done. Right next door I could drop in on my overachiever, who puts too much pressure on herself, and tell her to relax and not take her work too seriously. Paul was emphasizing one truth but not to the exclusion of another. He simply knew by the enlightenment of the Holy Spirit what message the Corinthians needed to hear.

As we read the Corinthians' mail, we need to remember who this letter was written to and why. This will help us understand and apply these truths in our own lives. Paul emphasized the powerful message of the cross and the downside of human wisdom. Verse 25 is a great summary statement: "This foolish plan of God is wiser than the wisest of human plans, and God's weakness is stronger than the greatest of human strength."

In what area of your life do you need wisdom right now?

Pause now and ask God for wisdom regarding your particular situation. We know from James 1:5 that God welcomes our requests: "If you need wisdom, ask our generous God, and he will give it to you. He will not rebuke you for asking." Take time to be still, inviting God to make His way clear to you through godly wisdom, not your own. Ask Him to use people, circumstances, and His Word to reveal or confirm any next steps you should take.

What I hear God saying to me:

What you hear may not make sense to you. God called Noah to build a boat, Hosea to marry a prostitute, and His only Son to die a painful death on a cross. Trust Him to lead you through whatever situation you are going through right now.

3. Boasting with Humility

After talking about the message of the cross and the futility of human wisdom, Paul went on to address a socially acceptable custom in Corinthian society: boasting. In Greco-Roman culture, students were schooled in the art of boasting about themselves. It was socially acceptable in government and business to use practiced rhetoric to speak about your best attributes and accomplishments. Boasting may have a negative connotation in our culture, but when it comes to resumes or bios we are taught to put our best face forward. I remember the first time I had to write my own bio, beginning "Melissa Spoelstra is…" It wasn't fun. It was explained to me that people want to know your background, including where you studied and your accomplishments, in order to decide quickly if they want to peruse what you've written. In reality, my bio could read, "Melissa Spoelstra is a sinner, saved only by grace. The only thing she has to boast about is that she knows Jesus."

Social media can be another place for a brag fest. While we can celebrate our family's accomplishments and milestones, we must be careful not to present ourselves to the world—virtual or otherwise—in a boastful way.

It's not wrong to identify our strengths and accomplishments and give God glory for the gifts and talents He has given each of us. Humility is not having a low view of self; it's recognizing our incredible value and worth because God thought us worth sacrificing His Son to save. So boasting in itself is not wrong, but the content of our boasting is critical.

Read 1 Corinthians 1:26-31 and count the number of times that the word *boast* is used. If you like, underline the word in your Bible whenever you encounter it. How many times is *boast* used in this passage?

What did Paul say many of the Corinthians were *not* like before God called them? (v. 26)

While we know that a government leader in Corinth named Erastus was a believer (Romans 16:23; 2 Timothy 4:20) and the city's former Jewish synagogue leader converted to Christianity (Acts 18:8), most of the believers were just regular folks.

Look again at verses 27-29. Why can't we boast in the presence of God?

Paul went on to give a gospel summary statement. Write your name in place of the pronouns by filling in the blanks in the following verse (see the next page):

"God has united _____ with Christ Jesus. For _____'s benefit God made him to be wisdom itself. Christ made _____ right with God; he made _____ pure and holy, and he freed _____ from sin."

(1 Corinthians 1:30)

Now read the verse aloud, soaking in the full effect of this statement. Write any thoughts or insights you have below:

God is a realist. He loves us so completely that He paid the ultimate price to free us from the penalty of sin, the power of sin, and—one day—the presence of sin.

In the last verse of the chapter, Paul quoted the prophet Jeremiah.

Therefore, as the Scriptures say, "If you want to boast, boast only about the LORD."
(1 Corinthians 1:31)

Read 1 Corinthians 1:31 in the margin. Then read the passage below, underlining the sentence that Paul echoes in 1 Corinthians 1:31:

²³ *This is what the Lord says:*

"Don't let the wise boast in their wisdom,

   or the powerful boast in their power,

   or the rich boast in their riches.

²⁴ *But those who wish to boast*

   should boast in this alone:

that they truly know me and understand that I am the Lord

   who demonstrates unfailing love

      and who brings justice and righteousness to the earth,

and that I delight in these things.

   I, the Lord, have spoken!"

(Jeremiah 9:23-24)

God doesn't want us to live with a distorted view of reality. He is the only One worth boasting about. He isn't a megalomaniac who is obsessed with people boasting about Him; He just favors the truth. One author expresses it well: "So the kindest thing God can do is to puncture sinful human pride and shatter the illusion of human self-sufficiency. He does that by using the obscure, weak, and foolish things to confound the strong and the wise."[13]

Later in his letter Paul would help the Corinthian believers work through some pretty serious issues including relational disagreements, doctrinal differences, and how to handle sexual sin in the church. But before answering their questions related to those issues, he helped them build a framework by learning to apply godly wisdom.

Rather than simply giving them answers, he wanted to be sure they recognized three truths that should be the starting blocks for every discussion or disagreement.

Write in your own words the three important truths we explored today:

1.

2.

3.

God used Paul to challenge the Corinthians with these concepts. They also hit home very practically with us. By keeping these three concepts in mind, we can find unity even in the midst of our diversity.

Talk with God

Remind yourself of these three important concepts throughout the day and evaluate how you might embrace them more fully as you approach your own relationship issues. Pray the guided prayer below or write your own prayer in the margin.

Lord, help me not to lose sight of the message of the cross. I'm so grateful that You died for my sins. Help me to see myself and others as holy and loved because of Your sacrifice. Many times I listen only to my own logic or allow worldly wisdom to creep into my life. Help me to remember that Your wisdom far exceeds any-thing I can come up with on my own. Jesus, help me not to boast about my job, financial status, ministry position, or any other accomplishment. Instead, help me to be grateful for all that You have provided and boast in You alone. Amen.

DAY 4: BEYOND IMAGINATION

Recently my son came home from college on the spur of the moment to surprise his little sister on her thirteenth birthday. When we sent her to the kitchen to get the cake, he jumped out and hugged her. Overcome

The places where we live shape us in ways we may not even realize. Check out the online Digging Deeper article for Week 1, "My Town," to discover how the town of Corinth shaped the original audience of Paul's first letter to the Corinthians (see AbingdonPress.com /FirstCorinthians).

Extra Insight

with emotion, she clung to him and cried. My other daughter captured it on video, and I have to admit I've watched it quite a few times. (Okay, maybe like thirty!) It makes me emotional to see them growing up and loving each other so fiercely, especially in light of the years of arguing and discord in our house. We are a family of debaters who like to get our own way. I treasure special moments like this when I get a glimpse into their love before they start bickering over who will get the biggest piece of cake. Most of life is hard, ordinary, and fraught with conflict, so we treasure the flickers of grace when we experience them.

As we open the second chapter of Paul's letter today, we will find him reminding the church that in the midst of their questions, factions, and difficulties, the mystery of God's incredible love and plan for the future should overshadow their doctrinal and relational skirmishes. Paul takes up right where he left off at the end of chapter 1, talking about not boasting in human wisdom.

> **Read 1 Corinthians 2:1-9 and note how Paul delivered the message when he was with them:**
>
> **He didn't come with** _____ **(vv. 1, 4)**
>
> **He came with** _____ **(v. 3)**
>
> **According to verse 5, why did Paul choose to preach the gospel in this manner?**

Remember that the Corinthians lived in a culture that worshiped knowledge, intelligence, and human wisdom. Eloquence and special insight could earn status or even fame in a town such as Corinth.

> **How do you think persuasive words or a demonstrative presentation actually could have been detrimental to the clarity of Paul's message? (Think about times when someone's eloquence was a distraction to you.)**

We've already learned this week that the believers in Corinth were prone to attach themselves to particular teachers. Paul didn't want to take anything away from the simple message of the gospel. It didn't need to be dressed up or made palatable or appealing. Let's consider how Paul's approach to the gospel can be applied in our own culture.

Do you think Paul is saying that we should never communicate the message of Jesus any way other than the plain method he used (nothing clever, articulate, or eloquent)? Explain your answer:

Paul says later in the letter that he tried to engage people in relevant ways by being all things to all people so that he might win some (1 Corinthians 9:19-23). So we need context and perspective to understand what Paul is saying here in chapter 2. These verses help us understand that Paul is asking us to know our audience. Rather than outlining a certain method that always is to be used when presenting the gospel, he is highlighting again the superiority of God's mysterious plan over human logic.

Paul reminds us that we don't need to "dress up" the simple message that God's mysterious plan included sending a Messiah to save us. God gave up His only Son to pay the price for all our sins and then raised Him from the dead to new life. Paul states clearly that he preached only "Christ and him crucified" (1 Corinthians 2:2 NIV). Yet Paul isn't saying that we shouldn't do things with excellence, be culturally relevant, or try to persuade people to follow Christ. Given the cultural appetite for knowledge and rhetoric, Paul simply had been careful not to be another teacher people were drawn to initially and then dismissed when they were ready to move on to someone or something else.

Jesus had modeled this straightforward approach to truth before Paul. He drew crowds when he stood up to injustice and talked about loving one's neighbor, but when he taught about eating his flesh and drinking his blood, the crowds began to dissipate (John 6:60-66). The disciples wondered if he should tone down the confusing or offensive teachings, but Jesus didn't come to entertain. He came to speak the truth and give His life for the church.

We certainly live in a culture that worships intelligence. While believing the gospel doesn't mean crucifying our intellect, it does mean taking a leap of faith. And as history reveals, a basic presentation of the gospel message is still effective. One commentator makes this observation:

> It is interesting to compare possibly the three greatest evangelists in North America during the last 150 years— D. L. Moody, Billy Sunday, and Billy Graham. Neither Moody nor Graham was known for impressing audiences with lofty rhetoric, frequently their sermons were deemed simplistic. Sunday was known for a flashy style, but he still preached a very basic gospel message. But all three centered on the cross and the need for personal conversion. As a result, they gave encouragement to millions of "down-and-outers," and countless came to the Lord through their preaching.[14]

What are some ways you have been able to share the gospel message with people in your sphere of influence? What has been effective?

It encourages me that Paul brought his weakness and willingness, and from there the church in Corinth was born.

Take a minute to read Acts 18:1-11 for some more insight into the Corinthian church plant. Answer the following questions:

What husband and wife team did Paul meet in Corinth? (vv. 1-2)

What was Paul's occupation in Corinth? (v. 3)

Where did Paul go initially to preach the gospel? (vv. 4-5)

How was Paul's gospel message received by the people worshiping in the Jewish synagogue? (v. 6)

Who then did Paul preach to? (vv. 6-8)

What message did Paul receive from the Lord in a vision? (vv. 9-10)

How long did Paul stay in Corinth? (v. 11)

What additional insights do you gain from this passage about why Paul chose a simple approach to preaching the gospel to the Gentiles?

Paul's vision encouraged him to stay the course in church planting. Though you may not have received a direct vision from the Lord as Paul did, how has God encouraged you to stay the course in spreading His love to others when you have been discouraged?

It's easy to get discouraged when people reject God's offer of love and salvation. If we aren't careful, our human tendency can be to feel that they are rejecting us along with God's message. The Lord offers Himself freely to everyone and uses us to tell others about His sacrifice on the cross and His love for all of humanity. However, we must continue to listen for His leading concerning when, how, and to whom we share our faith.

Paul faced rejection from most of his own people. While one of the synagogue leaders named Crispus converted to Christianity, as well as Titius Justus who was a Gentile proselyte to Judaism, Paul found more fertile ground for the gospel outside the Jewish community. These Gentile converts might have included workers who spent time alongside Paul, Aquila, and Priscilla on a daily basis. They could have included food vendors, shop workers, or those who unloaded the ships that were constantly passing through Corinth. They were regular folks who heard Paul preach the simple gospel message that Jesus had died for their sins. As we will see, the varied backgrounds of the church members played a role in the dissensions that Paul addressed in his letter.

Have you seen differences in upbringing, culture, and background cause challenges in relationships within the church? If so, how?

The power of the gospel can change any of us—from the most pious religious leader to the worldliest individual. Paul didn't want the Corinthian believers to lose sight of the common ground they shared despite their varied backgrounds. He reminded them in his letter that it wasn't fancy words that led them to decide to follow Jesus; it was the transforming power of the gospel message. God was so *for* them that He rescued them all from their sin by sending His Son to die in their place.

When I meditate on the truth of God's sacrificial love, I am overcome that God loves *me* that much. I have one son. He recently left for college, and I miss him. I can't imagine giving him up for anything—much less watching him suffer for the sake of others. Only a great and incredible love for us could motivate God to give up His perfect, sinless Son. That is how much God loves us. In the midst of all the junk of this life—the conflicts,

disagreements, and hardships—God wants to remind us that He is crazy about us. Even when life stinks, He is good.

As I've mentioned, Paul had spent eighteen months with the Corinthians and had been away from them for about three to five years when he wrote this letter. He knew from the tone of the letter they had written to him, asking questions, as well as the reports he had heard about their squabbles, that they needed a reminder of the goodness of God in the midst of the trials of life.

What about you? Do you need a reminder today of the goodness of God in the midst of your crazy life? Just as I need those glimpses of sweetness among my children, I also need gentle reminders from the Lord that He is for me, that He sees me, and that He has good plans ahead.

I once heard a preacher say that we are like fish out of water. The sea is heaven, and we are fish flopping around on the beach. Sometimes we feel like that, don't we? That analogy encourages me with the reminder that my struggles in this life are normal. I was made for heaven. With that in mind, I can look forward to all that God has in store in this life and the next.

If you were to imagine the best day possible, what sights and sounds would it include? How do you think your "best day" might compare to heaven?

Let's close by looking at the last verse of the section of Paul's letter we're studying today, where he cites another passage from Isaiah. I pray you will get a sweet reminder of God's great love for you and His good plans for your future.

Read 1 Corinthians 2:9 in the margin, and write it below in your own words:

However, as it is written:

"What no eye has seen,
what no ear has heard,
and what no human mind has conceived"—
the things God has prepared for those who love him—
(1 Corinthians 2:9 NIV)

Though Paul didn't write an exact quote of Isaiah, most commentators agree that he was drawing from a passage in Isaiah 64. While your perfect day might be a day at the beach or spa, God tells us His plans for us are greater than anything we could ask or imagine.

Now read Isaiah 64:1-4 below, underlining the phrases that are reminiscent of 1 Corinthians 2:9:

¹ *Oh, that you would burst from the heavens and come down!*

How the mountains would quake in your presence!

² *As fire causes wood to burn*

   and water to boil,

your coming would make the nations tremble.

   Then your enemies would learn the reason for your fame!

³ *When you came down long ago,*

   you did awesome deeds beyond our highest expectations.

   And oh, how the mountains quaked!

⁴ *For since the world began,*

   no ear has heard

and no eye has seen a God like you,

   who works for those who wait for him!

(Isaiah 64:1-4)

While Isaiah talks about those who "wait" and Paul talks about those who "love," the concept is that God has great things in store for us beyond our imagination. Paul says that we can't even wrap our minds around what God has planned for us! Revelation 21:4 tells us that heaven includes no tears, pain, or death. That is hard to imagine. In the meantime, God calls us to trust Him. We are to love Him and His church with our whole hearts and wait for the day when He returns or calls us home. But until then, He has purpose for us here.

Tomorrow we will finish chapter 2, which offers us encouragement related to how to "flop around on the beach" (live in this world of struggles) with intentionality and hope. Although the gospel may not be flashy, it certainly is beyond all we could ask or think. Let's end this day thanking God that our future with Him will go beyond our wildest dreams!

Talk with God

Read and meditate on these verses: John 14:2, 1 Thessalonians 4:16-17, and Revelation 21:3-4. Spend a few moments praising God that He is coming back to bring us into His presence forever.

DAY 5: A SPIRITUAL MIND

Yesterday we observed Paul reminding the Corinthian believers that God would knock their socks off in the future with things they couldn't even begin to imagine. While Paul's writings affirm that the Lord gives us His presence and so many wonderful blessings here on earth, his reference to the passage from Isaiah had a tone that smacked of that future day when Jesus will return.

So what are we to do here on earth until Jesus comes? Should we huddle up and wait it out? God gives us the hope of heaven to help us through the difficult times, but do we just grin and bear it, getting through the ups and downs of life the best we can? How do we know how to handle disagreements or doctrinal questions? Jesus is no longer on the earth in human form to correct and answer questions for his disciples. Paul and the original apostles are not here so that we may write letters to them when we are confused. In today's reading we will find some answers.

Read 1 Corinthians 2:10-16 and give one insight from each verse related to the Holy Spirit's role in our lives. I've done the first one for you.

Verse	Holy Spirit's Role
10	**The Spirit knows everything and helps us understand what God is doing.**
11	
12	
13	
14	
15	
16	

Here we see some of the great benefits of the Holy Spirit in our lives. Paul seems to be restating a similar theme in these verses.

How would you summarize in one sentence what Paul is trying to tell us about God's Holy Spirit?

As we continue to make our way through Paul's letter to the believers at Corinth, we will study more specifically the gifts of the Holy Spirit. He is the third person of the Godhead—not an impersonal force in our lives. Even though we don't have Jesus with us in human form so that we may ask Him questions to clarify issues, we have the Holy Spirit. Jesus said this about the Holy Spirit:

16 "And I will ask the Father, and he will give you another Advocate, who will never leave you. 17 He is the Holy Spirit, who leads into all truth. The world cannot receive him, because it isn't looking for him and doesn't recognize him. But you know him, because he lives with you now and later will be in you."

(John 14:16-17)

Paul's words in 1 Corinthians 2 line up with Christ's own words regarding the Spirit. Paul would go on to address relational, doctrinal, and practical issues. But before he did, he wanted to be sure the Corinthians were aware that they already had access to Someone far greater and wiser than he. He knew he would not always be around for them to write letters to when they didn't know how to handle certain situations. So he reminded them of the power of the Holy Spirit to guide them.

I'm thankful that God doesn't leave us to figure things out on our own, aren't you? He gives us His Spirit because He longs for us to know Him and be close to Him. Yet so easily we can become unaware of His presence, forgetting He is with us—and within us.

One time I was searching the house for something I needed for a conference. I finally had to make do without it. Later I was unpacking the van and found I had put it in the back of the vehicle so I wouldn't forget. Ugh!

I wonder if God feels the same tinge of frustration when we forget the gift of His Spirit, who lives inside us from the moment we choose to follow Him. Because of this gift, we have everything we need. As 2 Peter 1:3 tells us, "By his divine power, God has given us everything we need for living a godly life. We have received all of this by coming to know him, the one who called us to himself by means of his marvelous glory and excellence."

What are some of the ways the Holy Spirit helps us live a godly life? A primary role of the Holy Spirit is to illuminate God's Word and help us understand what God is like (John 14:26). I once heard someone say that memorizing God's Word increases the Holy Spirit's vocabulary in your life. I've found that to be true. In moments of doubt, God reminds me of Psalm 94:19: "When doubts filled my mind, / your comfort gave me renewed hope and cheer." When I am afraid, 2 Timothy 1:7 comes to mind: "For God has not given us a spirit of fear and timidity, but of power, love, and self-discipline." I find that the Holy Spirit brings God's Word to mind at just the right time.

Other times the Holy Spirit directs my thoughts, gives me discernment, gives me peace about a decision, inspires me with creative ideas, comforts me, tames my wild emotions, and illuminates sin in my heart.

The Scriptures tell us that the Holy Spirit comforts (John 14:26 KJV), teaches or guides (John 14:26; 16:13), equips (1 Corinthians 12:4-7), counsels (John 14:26), convicts (John 16:8), and reveals the future (John 16:13). We also learn about the role of the Spirit in Ephesians 5:18, where Paul contrasts being controlled by the Spirit with being drunk with wine. Similar to the way that wine alters the thinking, attitude, and actions of a person under its influence, the Spirit focuses our minds on God and helps us discern God's will for our daily circumstances.

Throughout church history as well as today, the role of the Holy Spirit has been a cause for spirited debate. However, as we look at Paul's words in 1 Corinthians 2, we can all agree that the Holy Spirit helps us understand spiritual things. Where human wisdom fails us, the Spirit gives us insight into our Father's heart.

Paul said the Holy Spirit shows us God's deep secrets (1 Corinthians 2:10). What are some ways the Holy Spirit has revealed things to you personally?

Later in the chapter, as he continues to teach about the Holy Spirit, Paul draws from the prophet Isaiah again, echoing these words from Isaiah 40:13: "Who is able to advise the Spirit of the Lord? / Who knows enough to give him advice or teach him?" Then Paul brings an answer to this didactic refrain with a great truth to encourage all who are indwelt by the Holy Spirit.

"Who has known the mind of the Lord so as to instruct him?"

But we have the mind of Christ.
(1 Corinthians 2:16 NIV)

Read Paul's words in 1 Corinthians 2:16 (in the margin). According to this verse, what do we possess?

Take that in for a minute. Say it out loud: "I have the mind of Christ."

When you think you'll never figure out what to do next, when you feel stuck in a relationship that seems will never change, when you lose all confidence about the direction of your life—allow the Holy Spirit to remind you that *you have the mind of Christ.* This realization should give us God-confidence, not arrogance.

Let's remember what the Scriptures tell us about the mind of Christ.

Read Philippians 2:5-8. What insights do these verses give us about what Christ's mind is like?

Having the mind of Christ should give us greater confidence, yet this confidence is coupled with the humble realization that the wisdom of the God of the universe resides in us through the Holy Spirit. If anyone ever had a reason to boast about His position and power, it would be Christ. Yet He took on the form of a servant, gave up His rights, and obeyed to the point of death. This is the "mind"—or attitude—that should govern our thinking and decisions. Whenever we are standing at a crossroads or facing a difficult situation, having the mind of Christ should cause us to consider questions such as these:

- How can I look out for the interests of others through this difficulty? (Philippians 2:4)
- What thoughts do I need to take captive to make them obedient to the ways of Christ? (2 Corinthians 10:5)
- What true, honorable, and praiseworthy things can I set my mind on? (Philippians 4:8)

What has been your state of mind recently? When you have quiet moments riding in the car, lying in bed at night, or going about your daily routine, where do your thoughts often land?

My mind often can be a battlefield. My thought life defaults to worry, judgment, and sometimes the land of "what if" or "if only." I must choose to redirect my thoughts and ask the Holy Spirit to take control. Surrendering to the humility of Christ in our minds requires us to be intentional.

What are some practices that help you stop an unhealthy thinking pattern and yield to the Holy Spirit's wisdom? Circle any below that you have found helpful:

Listening to uplifting music	**Changing your surroundings**
Meditating on Scripture	**Writing in your journal**
Going for a walk/run or exercising	**Calling an encouraging friend**
Thinking about a person in need	**Centering your thoughts on Christ**
Asking the Holy Spirit to help	**Praying for the situation or people**
Reciting a prayer, poem, or Scripture	**Reading a portion of Scripture**

What other ideas can you add to these?

As we continue our study of Paul's letter to the church in Corinth in the weeks to come, we will hit some tricky passages. We will need to unwrap their cultural practices and, more than likely, learn to lovingly disagree with others in the body of Christ concerning how we interpret and apply some of these passages. When we are tempted to be frustrated or throw in the towel, let's remember that we have the mind of Christ. He will give us understanding and reveal Himself to us as we seek Him wholeheartedly. As we draw near to Him and yield our lives to the control of the Holy Spirit, we will find His humility taking shape within us.

Talk with God

As a way of responding in prayer to all we've studied this week, share your thoughts in a letter of your own. In the space below, write a brief letter to God, praising Him for the cross, confessing any attitudes that are causing divisions in your own relationships, and thanking Him for the gifts of heaven, His Spirit, and the mind of Christ.

_____

_____

_____

_____

_____

_____

_____

_____

_____

_____

_____

WEEKLY WRAP-UP

This week we studied the first two chapters of Paul's letter by reading them in short sections so that we could focus on understanding each part. However, in using this approach we risk losing the flow of the letter, which was designed to be read out loud and passed among the house churches. So we will finish our study each week by reading in one sitting the chapters we've covered that week. This wrap-up exercise should take you approximately 6-7 minutes for reading the chapters and a few additional minutes for recording reflections.

Take a few minutes to read 1 Corinthians 1 and 2 again—either out loud if possible or silently if you are in a public setting. What new insights or applications did the Holy Spirit lift off the page as you read?

Here are some of the highlights from our study this week:

- Paul knew the Old Testament so well that he could quote Jeremiah and Isaiah and tie them into his message through the prompting of the Holy Spirit.
- Paul used repetition. He really wanted the Corinthians to understand the superiority of God's wisdom over human understanding.
- The message of the cross never ceases to overwhelm and amaze me. The fact that God sent His only Son for *me*!
- The hope of heaven and the Holy Spirit are gifts from God to help us through even our darkest days.

God's Word is alive and active. Paul's letter to a troubled church echoes into my life with such relevancy, and I pray it is resonating into yours as well!

IN CHRIST ALONE

_____ _____to God, so it should matter to us.

- Jesus prayed for our unity in the church. (John 17:20-23)

- Paul wrote about unity in his letters. (Romans 14:19, Ephesians 4:13, Colossians 3:14, 1 Corinthians 1:10)

I appeal to you, dear brothers and sisters, by the authority of our Lord Jesus Christ, to live in

_____ *with each other. Let there be no divisions in the church. Rather, be of one*

mind, _____ *in thought and purpose.*

(1 Corinthians 1:10)

Christ calls us to _____ not _____.

- Unity includes diversity.

- Uniformity eliminates diversity.

Realizing our _____ _____ in Christ gives us the starting point for dealing with disagreement.

- Those who have called on the name of Christ are holy. (1 Corinthians 1:2)

How would that change us—if we looked at the people we disagree with and began to see them as _____?

- We should value and treasure people because they are loved by God and are holy.

VIDEO VIEWER GUIDE: WEEK 1

A New H_2O

H_1 = _____

- We can't imagine what God has prepared for us in heaven. (1 Corinthians 2:9)
- When discerning what to do in a situation, we need to ask ourselves, "Is this going to matter in heaven?"

H_2 = _____

- God has given us His Holy Spirit to guide and lead us. (1 Corinthians 2:11-12)
- We have the mind of Christ. (1 Corinthians 2:16)

O = _____

- We can have joy knowing that the hope of heaven and the Holy Spirit will never change.

Week 2

GROWING UP

1 Corinthians 3–5

For the Kingdom of God is not just a lot of talk; it is living by God's power.
(1 Corinthians 4:20)

DAY 1: WORDS OF WARNING

A friend I'll refer to as Renee called to tell me how frustrated she was with a situation regarding her sister. Six months ago her sister had called to ask Renee to hold her accountable in her renewed pursuit to follow Jesus. After a recent divorce, she had wanted to get her life back on track and incorporate some spiritual disciplines such as going to church, joining a Bible study, and spending more time in prayer. This same sister now had called to say she was moving in with a new boyfriend. She also admitted that she had not taken action in any of the areas where she had asked for accountability, even though Renee had lovingly checked in with her several times over the months.

The last thing Renee wanted to do was judge or shame her sister, yet she believed her sister's recent decision would not fill her emptiness and longings but instead would take her down a harmful path. Renee struggled with whether to warn her sister of potential problems or simply listen. After praying about it, she decided to remind her sister of the commitment she had made six months before and then share some of her concerns. When Renee asked me what I thought of her decision, I empathized with the predicament of not knowing when to give words of caution and when to silently love and pray.

Many of us have been unsure of how to love others with truth that doesn't carry the weight of judgment. The Apostle Paul surely knew this struggle as he carefully chose his words and attempted to help the believers in Corinth mature in faith. Though our study today is in 1 Corinthians 3, let's jump ahead briefly to chapter 4 and look at a verse that provides a framework for understanding Paul's heart behind his words.

Read 1 Corinthians 4:14 in the margin. According to this verse, what was not Paul's intent in writing?

What was his true motive?

We all get off track in our faith journeys at times, making bad decisions that bring varying consequences into our lives. So when we see immaturity

Extra Insight

Some leaders of the early church, such as Tertullian and Hippolytus, had a custom of supplying a drink of milk to newly baptized converts.[1] This symbolized that the individuals were now baby Christians unable to feed themselves yet and in need of nourishment from the community of faith.

I am not writing these things to shame you, but to warn you as my beloved children.
(1 Corinthians 4:14)

or sin in the lives of other believers and feel led by God's Spirit to lovingly address it, we must be careful to clearly communicate our motive for offering caution before offering words of correction.

Recall a time when you were corrected or admonished by another believer. Did you feel the person was issuing words of warning in love or shaming you in judgment? Explain your response.

Read 1 Corinthians 3:1-9 and answer the following questions: To what did Paul compare the Corinthian believers? (vv. 1-2)

What reason did he give for calling them infants? (v. 3)

What was the source of their fighting? (vv. 4-5)

We find here that the source of their fighting was related to their comparison of their leaders, just as we saw Paul mention in the early paragraphs of his letter (see 1 Corinthians 1:12). Rather than focusing on God, who makes seeds grow, they were arguing over who was a better planter or waterer.

We might be tempted to think this example does not relate to us if we are not dividing into factions, but the underlying principle Paul was making has much broader application.

Think about the last argument or disagreement you had (whether with a spouse, child, coworker, ministry partner, extended family member, friend, or neighbor). What was the source of contention?

One of my recent disagreements seemed so important in the moment. I was sure I knew the faster way for Sean and me to get to our destination. In hindsight, it turned out to be a petty thing to be quarrelling over since the argument over the route overshadowed our enjoyment of the destination.

Read 1 Corinthians 3:3 and James 4:1-3. What themes do these passages have in common?

Paul told the Corinthians that their quarrels and jealousy revealed they were being controlled by their sinful nature. James said to his readers that they had evil (sinful) desires at war within them, which caused them to quarrel and be jealous of others. Paul concluded that the Corinthians were living like people of the world, and James observed that his readers wanted only what would give them pleasure. Like Paul and James, every spiritual leader must be able to lovingly speak truth in order to help those he or she is nurturing in the faith.

Rather than calling his brothers and sisters in Christ spiritual infants in a derogatory or condemning way, Paul was cautioning them in love. He knew the truth that is expressed in Romans 8:6: "So letting your sinful nature control your mind leads to death. But letting the Spirit control your mind leads to life and peace." Those are pretty high stakes! Like a parent who doesn't let a young child play in the street, Paul was a spiritual father who warned his children of the consequences of comparing, fighting, and making people into idols. His words show us that living love sometimes means telling people what they *need* to hear rather than what they *want* to hear.

Describe a time when someone spoke words you needed to hear— even if you didn't appreciate them initially:

I would imagine that as the Corinthians heard this letter read aloud, it stung a little. Those who had favored Apollos or Peter possibly scrunched down in their chairs. They may have felt targeted or insulted. Paul loved the Corinthians enough to give them what they needed rather than just what would make them feel good in the moment.

We have become so fragile in the church today. There are people who, when given any words of admonition—even from leaders with sincere motives—stomp away angrily, gossip to others, leave out crucial details, claim spiritual abuse, assume a victim mentality, or run away to another body of believers (until someone there admonishes them in some way, and then they move on again).

Of course, it is important to acknowledge that some leaders abuse their authority by manipulating, shaming, and controlling people. We see abuses of power throughout church history. Although there continue to be instances of abuse and control today, is it possible that, generally speaking,

we Christians in the West (both leaders and followers) have swung to the opposite extreme, overlooking sin more often than lovingly addressing it?

When I correct my teenagers, often I get a defensive, argumentative response that causes sparks to fly. It's easier to just turn the other way and pretend I don't see areas of weakness that need to be addressed. At times I'd rather pick up the socks on the living room floor, ignore the sibling fighting, and hope that someone else will teach them to grow up. (Can anyone relate?) In the same way, it can be easier to turn a blind eye to spiritual immaturity in our sisters and brothers in Christ than to risk relationship drama in our lives. Though we are not called to give unsolicited advice to every believer we know, at times God calls us to lovingly warn others who openly identify themselves as Christ-followers. Tim Keller says it this way, "Love without truth is sentimentality; it supports and affirms us but keeps us in denial about our flaws."[2] However, we should keep in mind that Paul had a relationship with the church at Corinth based on love and trust. In the same way, we must earn the right to give correction through relationship.

> **When giving a word of warning, what are some practical ways we can seek to be more loving so that we don't come across as shaming or judging? (Consider specifics related to timing, method, tone, and so on.)**

One of the women in the pilot group for this study mentioned that when a friend confides in her about personal problems, she asks this question to ascertain how she should respond: "Do you need a warm blanket or sandpaper right now?" She explained to the group that the warm blanket represents listening, understanding, and support, while the sandpaper represents gentle truth, pointed questions, and possible next steps. Though we may be led by God to speak a loving warning to someone we have relationship with, even when she or he doesn't want to hear it, asking permission before offering advice can help open the hearer's receptivity. When individuals express that they aren't ready to receive sandpaper when we offer it, we can let them know we are available if and when they do want to hear our cautions and then pray for another opportunity.

Here are a few important things to note about the warnings or admonitions made by Paul throughout his letter:

- Paul had a real relationship with the Corinthians; he was not writing as a stranger.
- Paul wrote as someone in authority; he had planted the church and was considered their spiritual father.

- Paul's comments were not unsolicited; the church had asked for advice with specific questions in a previous letter.
- Paul backed up general observations with tangible examples, offering solution-oriented specifics rather than broad criticisms (for example, after comparing them to spiritual infants, he gave them specific examples to help them understand more clearly what they needed to do).

We can offer words of correction as a friend or spiritual mentor, asking for permission before speaking, but our words will be useless if we fail to offer solution-oriented specifics.

When my twins were in the three-year-old classroom at church and I would come to pick them up after the service, the Sunday school teacher would often tell me how bad they had been in class. Needless to say, I dreaded the end of the church service. I asked the teacher for some examples so that I could address their behavior, but she never gave me specifics. I was told they were just generally naughty. This was frustrating as a mom, so I did the mature thing and started having my husband pick them up from class! I'll never forget the agony I felt upon receiving general criticism without concrete instances.

Paul didn't leave any room for confusion or uncertainty about the immaturity he observed in the Corinthian believers. He talked plainly about their jealousy, quarreling, and leader comparisons. We would be wise to follow his example.

Let's take a closer look at the flip side and consider what it's like when we are the ones receiving corrective words. Though I was receptive and wanted more information when the Sunday school teacher told me that the twins were behaving badly in class, that is not always my response when I am on the receiving end of correction—whether it pertains to my children or myself. In fact, sometimes the "Momma Bear" in me can rise up when other parents point out my children's flaws. It's okay for me to correct their laziness and sassiness, but I must admit that I get defensive when others bring attention to it. Likewise, when someone brings an area of personal spiritual weakness to my attention, my initial reaction is often defensive. However, with some time and prayer, I am ultimately grateful for it.

Read Psalm 141:5 in the margin. What does the psalmist compare godly correction to in this verse?

How is the Lord calling you to take this posture in a current situation right now?

Extra Insight

3 Guidelines for Receiving Criticism

1. Consider the source.
2. Ask God to confirm the areas pointed out.
3. Look for a nugget of truth—even if the claims seem exaggerated.

*Let the godly strike me!
It will be a kindness!
If they correct me, it is
soothing medicine.
Don't let me
refuse it.*
(Psalm 141:5)

I pray Psalm 141:5 will be our attitude toward those who issue words of warning when they see us headed down a dangerous path. One way I practice this verse is to give people who love me permission to speak into my life, especially when they see me going off course. I have asked several close friends and mentors to be on the lookout for pride, fear, and people-pleasing in my life. I know these are my tendencies, and they can creep into my thinking, words, and decisions when I least expect them. I am grateful to have people in my life who love me enough to speak gentle words of correction.

The Corinthians had that kind of spiritual mentor in Paul. As we've noted, they had asked him to give them advice. They had written him a letter, imploring him to help them deal with their problems. Though calling them spiritual infants may appear harsh, Paul had been invited into their lives as a spiritual father.

Who might you invite to help you when you get off course spiritually? List below a few people you could ask to be on the lookout for specific "sin tendencies" in your life:

Extra Insight

The Corinthians weren't the only church that struggled with growth. The author of the letter to the Hebrews admonished the Jewish believers for living on milk when they should have been eating spiritual solid food (see Hebrews 5:12-14).

If you struggle to embrace corrective words, ask God to give you the attitude of the psalmist who saw correction as soothing medicine. Most medicine doesn't taste good going down, but it helps us on the road to healing and growth.

As we learn to give cautions with love and receive correction without offense, we can take steps toward seeing one another as partners instead of competitors. While we may disagree in peripheral areas, we are called to work together in planting seeds of God's love among those who don't know Him. At times we will water the plants that have grown from gospel seeds sown by others. Whether we plant or water, the Lord calls us to remember that we are to work as partners, and that He alone is the One who causes growth.

Talk with God

The believers in Corinth struggled to get off spiritual milk, and it can be a problem for us, too. Spend some time in God's presence, asking how you can progress from being fed, to feeding yourself, to helping feed others. Invite Him to reveal any blind spots you may have that are inhibiting you from moving on to maturity in your spiritual diet.

DAY 2: FIREPROOF

I love to watch television shows where people take an old house with dilapidated structures and outdated décor and turn it into something beautiful. You know, the Lord wants to do a similar work in our broken lives, turning them into spiritual structures that reflect His glory. Today in our study of 1 Corinthians 3:10-23, we'll find Paul using buildings as an illustration of our Christian life. Paul challenged the Corinthians to be discerning and intentional with their design and materials.

Read 1 Corinthians 3:10-15 and fill in the areas below:

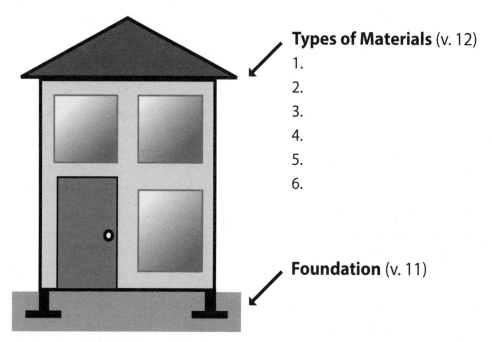

Types of Materials (v. 12)

1.
2.
3.
4.
5.
6.

Foundation (v. 11)

Extra Insight

The remains of the sixth-century B.C. temple of Apollo still stand today in Corinth.[3]

Let's reflect together on two principles we find in this illustration.

1. The foundation is critical.

We've just identified Christ as the foundation. Let's look at a few passages to see what further insights or confirmation they offer.

Read the following verses and fill in the chart, indicating who was speaking, what the passage is about, and how it relates to the foundation.

Passage	Person speaking	Summary statement	What it says about the foundation
Matthew 7:24-27			

"The foundation
is the most
important part
of the building
because it
determines the
size, shape, and
strength of the
superstructure."[4]

Passage	Person speaking	Summary statement	What it says about the foundation
John 5:39			
Acts 4:11-12			

These passages support the truth that Jesus must be our foundation!

Most modern homes are made of concrete. Something rock solid is needed to support a home through all kinds of weather and years of soil settlement—not to mention the traffic of people walking, playing, and living on top of that foundation. Christ is called the cornerstone (Acts 4:11-12) to assure us that when we make Him the foundation of our lives, we are standing on solid ground.

What are some things that people sometimes build their lives on other than Christ?

Jesus never changes. So when He is our foundation, we don't have to worry about cracks, rot, termites, storms, or anything life throws at us. We might need to make some repairs occasionally, but as a song I learned as a child says, a house built on the rock of Christ will not go splat when the rains come down and the floods come up! Jesus said the fool builds a house upon the sand instead of the rock (see Matthew 7:24-27). If we make our physical health, accumulation of wealth, talents, popularity, or outward appearance the basis for living, the storms of life will shake us to the core.

Paul wrote to the church at Corinth not to shame them but to warn them about the consequences of building on any foundation other than Christ alone.

Read 1 Corinthians 3:10 in the margin. How did Paul refer to himself?

According to the grace of God given to me, like a skilled master builder I laid a foundation, and someone else is building on it. Each builder must choose with care how to build on it. (1 Corinthians 3:10 NRSV)

Paul called himself a master builder. The Greek word is *architeckton*, which is where our word *architect* finds its root. However, this word carries with it the connotation of builder *and* designer.[5] Paul's specialty was foundations. His ministry focused largely on church plants and evangelism. On one of his missionary journeys he preached at the Jewish synagogue in Corinth and then to the Gentiles in the city. He reminded the church body to keep Christ at the foundation of everything they continued to do in his absence (Acts 18:1-6).

We cannot divorce 1 Corinthians 3:10-15 from its community focus. One commentator points out that all of Paul's metaphors refer to the community of believers. So the building here is representative of much more than the spiritual life of one person; it represents "the church community as a whole."[6] In the body of Christ, our common task of building things that will last for all eternity should take priority over disputable details. Yet within our local communities of faith, we can easily get distracted from Christ alone and build a foundation on things such as a leader's dynamic personality, a secondary issue, attractive methods or models, church tradition, or the moral teachings of Jesus (apart from the gospel). All of these dynamics are important to our faith, but they cannot be the foundation of any church.

Read Colossians 1:18 in the margin. What does this verse tell us?

No church is perfect. Although Christ is the foundation, the builders are human. Like the leaders at Corinth—and even Paul the master builder— we all struggle against sinful tendencies. In our own churches, expressions of worship and community are as varied as our creative God, but our foundation should be one and the same: Christ alone.

We may have relational difficulties or doctrinal differences within the body of Christ—and in fact, we disagree in many areas. Just read any Christian blog and the responses in the comments section! But in the midst of our struggles and disagreements, we can stand together on the firm foundation of Christ, helping one another build toward things that will echo into eternity.

Take a moment to reflect on this first principle. How does recognizing that Christ is the firm foundation for all believers affect your thinking about our differences?

2. The materials matter.

After we make Christ the foundation of our lives, we are not instantly "beamed up" to heaven—though on some days we might wish it happened

Christ is also the head of the church,
    which is his body.
He is the beginning,
    supreme over
    all who rise from
    the dead.
    So he is first in
    everything.
(Colossians 1:18)

In the midst of our struggles and disagreements, we can stand together on the firm foundation of Christ, helping one another build toward things that will echo into eternity.

that way! Throughout the rest of our days, God helps us learn from our mistakes, conforms us to His image, and uses us to help others find the Cornerstone in their own lives.

We learn through Paul's building illustration that our daily decisions echo into eternity. Where we invest our time, talents, and treasures will be tested with fire on Judgment Day. That can be a heavy and sobering thought, but let's be sure we don't misunderstand.

Look back to 1 Corinthians 3:13-15. What is the worst thing that can happen to a believer?

The loss of the worker who built poorly is a loss of rewards, not a loss of life. Those of us who have Christ as our foundation will be saved regardless of our work. The blood of Christ covers our sin—even if we have built everything on top of our foundation with shoddy materials. So this illustration of fire testing our building materials refers to a rewards judgment. If our work is burned up, we will experience loss in the form of a lack of rewards to present to Christ. This great loss will be the result of mismanaged time and opportunities.

Romans 8:1 puts it simply but powerfully: "So now there is no condemnation for those who belong to Christ Jesus." This verse refers not only to condemnation in the present time but also for all time. When Christ is our foundation, we can be sure of our life in eternity. But that should not lead us to think, "Whew! Then I can just live however I want, knowing that I will escape through the flames of a wasted life!"

Read Matthew 6:19-20 in the margin. How did Jesus call us away from this posture? What did He tell us to do?

Jesus calls us to make investments that will last forever. Though John had not penned the Revelation at the time of Paul's letter to Corinth, we find confirmation there that this rewards judgment will come to pass. Christ himself speaks of it.

Read Revelation 22:12 in the margin. Knowing that when Christ returns we will stand together at a rewards judgment, how does that motivate you to spend your time, talent, and treasure differently? Is there something specific the Lord is bringing to mind?

19 "Don't store up treasure here on earth, where moths eat them and rust destroys them, and where thieves break in and steal. 20 Store your treasures in heaven, where moths and rust cannot destroy, and thieves do not break in and steal."
(Matthew 6:19-20)

"Behold, I am coming quickly, and My reward is with Me, to render to every man according to what he has done."
(Revelation 22:12 NASB)

One commentator has noted that typical homes in Corinth were made from the combustible materials mentioned in these verses: "The frames of ordinary houses and buildings were built of wood; hay or dried grass, mixed with mud, was used for the walls; and roofs were thatched with straw or stalks."[8] Paul isn't saying that wood, hay, and stubble are bad; they are just ordinary. God calls us to live differently than everyone else. We won't build lasting spiritual homes with hours of television, scrolling through social media feeds, or wandering through shopping malls looking for more stuff. Many people build their lives with these ordinary things. Instead, the Lord calls us to build a life with rare and difficult-to-obtain materials.

What do you think these rare and difficult-to-obtain materials might be? What practices, thoughts, or attitudes are like gold, silver, or jewels?

As I think about building with things that will last, I am reminded of the words of my pastor when I was a teenager. He said that only two things will last forever: the Word of God and the souls of people. When I think of things that are precious, it usually involves people:

- Reading a book to a child
- Driving a friend who doesn't own a car to church
- Praying for those who are sick or struggling
- Laughing with dear friends
- Consoling my kids as they cry over teenage drama
- Listening to a colleague who is facing a difficult challenge

It's all about relationships! That's what will matter in eternity. Relationships aren't easy. They are complicated, messy, and unpredictable. We need prayer, perseverance, and God's supernatural grace to help us navigate them. Yet they are what matter most.

The temples of the Greek gods and the Jewish synagogues in Corinth were designed and decorated much differently than common homes. These were the places in the city where gold, silver, and precious stones could be found. Warren Wiersbe created this chart to help us contrast these types of materials from a Corinthian's perspective:[9]

Gold, Silver, Precious Stones	Wood, Hay, Stubble
Permanent	Passing, temporary
Beautiful	Ordinary, even ugly
Valuable	Cheap
Hard to obtain	Easy to obtain

As you look at this chart, what actions, attitudes, and ideas could you catalog from your own life as having these same qualities? Identify two habits or actions—or two uses of time, talent, or treasure—that you think would be combustible, or burned in the fire. Then identify two that would be fireproof.

Combustible	Fireproof

At times I can become lazy in pursuing wisdom and investing in eternal things. Those hours of playing online games, worrying about things I can't control, and even updating my house or wardrobe will "burn up" in eternity. Combustible things aren't necessarily bad—they are just ordinary and have no value in the next life. I often ask God to stamp eternity in my eyes so that I don't lose sight of the things that will last forever—the things that are fireproof. One of the most fireproof things we can do is help others draw close to God.

Knowing that if our work survives we will receive a reward but if it is burned up we will suffer great loss as someone escaping through flames, we should invest our time building relationships, sharing the gospel message, and praying for others. Even better than the reward we will receive is knowing that our efforts will help draw others to God so that they too may experience His saving grace.

Read Ephesians 2:8-10 in the margin. What do these verses tell us about salvation?

Underline the last sentence in this passage. Why are we made new in Christ?

8 God saved you by his grace when you believed. And you can't take credit for this; it is a gift from God. 9 Salvation is not a reward for the good things we have done, so none of us can boast about it. 10 For we are God's masterpiece. He has created us anew in Christ Jesus, so we can do the good things he planned for us long ago. (Ephesians 2:8-10)

I love how these two verses succinctly sum up our two principles today about foundations and materials. Salvation is by grace alone; it is a gift from God that comes through Christ. Even so, God has planned for us to do good things. These works do not earn our ticket to heaven; we were *created to do them*. We are His masterpiece—created for His purposes!

It certainly can be easy to get sucked into our self-centered, self-directed culture that wants everything to be easy and then forget about God's master plan. We live in a world of quick everything—from food to communication to spiritual disciplines. The question we must ask ourselves is, *How are all these quick, shoddy materials working for us?*

What is one small change that would help you build with quality materials in your spiritual life this week?

> **God puts His work on display in our lives, showing how He redeems us and makes us new.**

As we build together, don't be discouraged by the state of your house right now. Whether it's demolition day and you are ripping out carpet and rotted walls, or you're getting closer to the end of construction and putting on finishing touches, remember that God takes our brokenness and creates something beautiful. God puts His work on display in our lives, showing how He redeems us and makes us new.

Psalm 127:1a reminds us, "Unless the LORD builds a house, / the work of the builders is wasted." So let's end our time today talking with and listening to the ultimate Master Builder!

Talk with God

As you reflect on today's lesson, what do you hear God's Spirit saying to you? Ask God how He wants you to invest in what's eternal—people and His Word. Spend some time listening, and record any ideas that come to mind in the margin. Continue to pray about how you can build a fire-proof life and store your treasure in heaven.

DAY 3: LESS TALK, MORE ACTION

On a recent flight, my mother had a conversation with a man who had studied Greek language and history in college. Having served as a missionary in Eastern Europe, my mom has traveled to many Greek cities and was fascinated to hear more about his experiences. Yet when she asked what Greek cities he had visited, she was amazed to learn that he had never been to Greece. He knew a lot about Greek language, history, and customs, but he had not actually stepped foot on Greek soil.

In chapter 4, Paul admonishes the Corinthians for knowing information but struggling to put feet to their faith. He warns the church about talking big but living small. I can definitely relate, can't you? We talk the God talk but don't always walk the God walk. We fill our heads with information about the Bible, Jesus, and the Christian life, but sometimes our actions

When it comes to spiritual things, we can be educated beyond our obedience.

don't reflect the truths we claim to know. When it comes to spiritual things, we can be educated beyond our obedience. We need less talk, more action.

As we will see, Paul's tone and style in this chapter shift from sarcasm to compassion to irony and admonition. But if we can see past Paul's writing style to the heart of what he is saying, we will find truths we need to hear. As you read, remember from yesterday's lesson that real love is willing to confront gently and with grace.

Read 1 Corinthians 4:1-7 and then complete the chart below:

Verse	Word (or phrase) Paul used to describe himself and Apollos:	What they were put in charge of:
1		
2		

Before we dig into these two verses, a note of clarification is helpful. Paul is speaking in these verses of those who serve as leaders in the church, using himself and Apollos as examples. Today we often think of church leaders as ministers or "professional Christians" who preach, officiate at weddings and funerals, visit the sick, and oversee meetings. But the church at that time consisted of a fledgling body of believers without much official structure or organization. As Ray Stedman writes, "A minister of Christ in the New Testament church was anyone—and I mean literally *anyone*—who, by virtue of a gift of the Spirit, was a preacher or teacher of the Word of God."[10] So as we take a deeper look into what Paul was saying, we should consider ourselves ministers of the gospel—whether we teach Sunday school, lead a Bible study, shepherd our children in prayers or devotions, or share God's Word with others in any capacity. No ordination or degree is necessary to apply this passage in our lives!

The first word Paul used of himself and Apollos was *servant*, which brings us to our first insight from today's text.

1. "Less talk, more action" means being a servant.

As Christ-followers, we are to take the posture of the lowliest of servants. William Barclay gives us insight into the Greek word Paul chose for himself in verse 1, noting: "The word that he uses for a *servant* is interesting; it is *huperetes* and originally meant a rower on the lower bank of a trireme, one of the slaves who pulled at the large sweeps which moved the great ships of war through the sea."[11] Corinth was a port city where the Roman Empire docked their warships, so Paul knew his audience would be familiar with the concept of under-rowers.

Paul was claiming that as a minister of the gospel, he held the lowest position of an under-rower. He did the bidding of his Master rather than

Extra Insight

"When a Roman general won a great victory, he was allowed to parade his victorious army through the streets of the city with all the trophies that he had won; the procession was called a Triumph. But at the end, there came a little group of captives who were doomed to death."[12]

promote himself as someone great. A servant of Christ had been put in charge of explaining "God's mysteries." Most commentators agree that Paul was referring to the gospel of Christ. The under-rower was the lowliest of servants in Corinthian culture, so Paul was saying that the lowliest of servants had been charged with the greatest message.

Jesus showed us the importance of servant leadership when he washed his disciples' feet at the last supper (John 13:1-17). The servant who had the job of foot washing was on par with the work of an under-rower. The lowliest of jobs are often the most vital, and we must not think ourselves too important to get our hands dirty.

Having wealth, extensive education, or special talents and abilities are certainly not sinful. However, we must remember that whatever we have comes from God. Paul asked the Corinthians, "What do you have that God hasn't given you?" (1 Corinthians 4:7). We must consider this question as well.

Identify one or two of God's gifts—whether material things or abilities—that might tempt you toward pride if you were to forget where they came from:

Spend a few minutes talking to the Lord right now. Ask Him to help you remember that every ability and talent you possess comes from Him. Thank God for His example of servant leadership, and pray that God would help you take a posture of service that would be evident to others in your life today.

2. "Less talk, more action" means being a steward.

In verse 2 we find another illustration to help us understand what it means to lead by putting our faith in action. Though we operate as a servant who answers to Christ, we also have been given authority to lead as a *steward*. A steward is one who has oversight and responsibility while operating under the authority of a master. Some translations use the word *steward* (NKJV, NASB, NRSV, ESV), while others use the word *manager* (NLT, CEB) or the phrase "those who have been given a trust" (NIV).

One commentator explains that the Greek word used here for steward "was employed to denote 'a confidential slave to whom a master entrusted the direction of his house, and in particular the care of distributing to all the servants their tasks and provision.' "[13] This person was a servant who had authority over the other servants. I think of Joseph in the Old Testament, for example, who was a servant under Potiphar in a position of authority.

A *trireme* was a Roman warship where the ship's power came from under-rowers— slaves or prisoners in chains rowing together.

Read Luke 12:42-43 in the margin. Circle the word *servant* **and underline the word** *master*. **How does our Lord describe a faithful servant?**

As stewards, God has given us resources, people, and bodies to oversee. Yet we can become so focused on the flaws of others that we neglect to manage what God has given us. It is easy to criticize how others are mismanaging their time, money, and health. Instead, God calls us to keep our eyes on Him, knowing that we will give a personal account to God alongside our leaders and other believers.

How are you stewarding God's resources in the following areas? Put an X on the line to indicate where you fall in regard to each statement:

1. Health

I'm eating and exercising in a way that enables me to use my body to serve God and others.

_____

Strongly Agree   Agree   Disagree   Strongly Disagree

2. Finances:

I'm saving, spending, and giving in a way that honors God and helps further His kingdom.

_____

Strongly Agree   Agree   Disagree   Strongly Disagree

3. Time management

I'm using my time in a way that is directed by the Holy Spirit— incorporating work, rest, service, and play with an emphasis on relationships.

_____

Strongly Agree   Agree   Disagree   Strongly Disagree

4. Talents

I'm using the gifts and abilities God has entrusted to me to serve others.

_____

Strongly Agree   Agree   Disagree   Strongly Disagree

Ouch. That wasn't a fun activity for me. But let's not live with a focus on our weaknesses; instead, let's look for ways we can better steward the resources God has given us.

In which of these four areas do you sense God calling you to make the most significant stewardship changes? Circle the area and write a one-sentence prayer, asking for God's help as you manage His resources.

Body/health   Finances   Time   Talents

_____

God calls us to stop looking at others' lives through the microscope of judgment and start looking in the mirror, focusing on our own stewardship issues. Romans 14:4 echoes Paul's words in 1 Corinthians 4:5 regarding our need to focus on ourselves instead of others.

Read 1 Corinthians 4:5 and Romans 14:4 in the margin. Why are we to keep our focus on our own service rather than the decisions of others?

We've seen that in the first two verses of 1 Corinthians 4, Paul used common vernacular for an under-rower and an overseer to emphasize two key points of service: 1) Spiritual leaders should not see themselves as overly important but humbly serve Christ with a willingness to do whatever He asks; 2) Followers should not judge their leaders' motives, because those in authority will answer to Christ alone for their leadership.

Now, reread 1 Corinthians 4:3-4. What does Paul say about being judged?

Paul says he isn't concerned with what others think about him! I admit this is a tough one for me. I've fought a people-pleasing problem my whole life. What about you?

How does being reminded that we shouldn't use the approval of human authority as our primary gauge resonate with you?

So don't make judgments about anyone ahead of time—before the Lord returns. For he will bring our darkest secrets to light and will reveal our private motives. Then God will give to each one whatever praise is due.
(1 Corinthians 4:5)

Who are you to condemn someone else's servants? Their own master will judge whether they stand or fall. And with the Lord's help, they will stand and receive his approval.
(Romans 14:4)

I hope it brings a measure of freedom as you align with Paul's attitude.

Note also that Paul said he didn't even trust his own judgments. The Stoic philosophers in Corinth taught that self-examination was the most important measuring tool in life.[14] Being confident and happy with yourself was all that mattered. That statement connects with mainstream American thinking, doesn't it? The undertones in commercials, movies, and even some of the things my kids bring home from school communicate that we need to please only ourselves. Paul warned against self-evaluation as the sole means of decision-making by saying he realized that his own perspective could be skewed. We need a multitude of sources when making judgments. God's Word, feedback from others, impressions in prayer, and our own thoughts must all be used to get a more complete picture.

Why do you think Paul taught that we can't trust our own view of ourselves?

The truth is that we all are biased! Sometimes I see only my perspective. I can try to put myself in others' shoes, but I can't possibly know what it's really like to live another person's life. Paul isn't saying we should never consider the thoughts of others or do some self-evaluation; he is reminding us that it is the Lord Himself who will examine us.

What is God saying to you about how you judge others or yourself in regard to spiritual progress?

Now, let's see how Paul applied these truths to the Corinthian believers and learn what we can apply in our own circumstances.

Read 1 Corinthians 4:8-13, and fill in the chart below, noting how Paul said the apostles responded in these situations:

Verse	When others do this	We respond like this
12a	Curse, revile	
12b	Persecute, abuse	
13	Slander, defame, say evil things	

How do the apostles' responses in these verses reveal a walk that matches a talk?

It's important to note that Paul wasn't saying we should allow others to treat us harshly and forget all relationship boundaries. He doesn't ask us to enable or excuse abuse. Paul even stood up for himself in court when he had an opportunity (see Acts 22:1, 25). But even so, there are times when we are unable to avoid the mistreatment of others. Sometimes we have no choice except our posture.

I've heard it said that the true test of a servant is how one responds when he or she is treated like one. Paul wasn't commanding the Corinthian believers to allow others to treat them poorly; he was reminding them that following Christ means choosing an attitude of Christlike humility. Writing about this passage, one commentator observed, "The image of the suffering apostle should be held clearly before our eyes, and then we should ask ourselves: Are we sure we want to belong to Christ and share his way?"[15] The Corinthians had begun to view the Christian life as synonymous with achievement and privilege instead of service and humility—which can be a real danger for us as well. Paul used irony and scathing sarcasm in these verses to communicate this important question: "Do we or don't we follow a crucified Messiah who asked us to take up our own crosses and follow Him?"

As we address the need for our walk to match our talk, facing suffering or persecution can be a litmus test for us. Like hot water brings out what's inside a tea bag, the hot water of trials can reveal what's really going on inside of us—and sometimes it can be pretty dark.

What has a time of suffering or persecution revealed about your faith?

We see an abrupt change in tone as the chapter ends. Paul makes use of shock value and irony to hold the Corinthians' attention as he closes with comments about something he knew was integral to their spiritual growth.

Read 1 Corinthians 4:15-21. What did Paul ask the Corinthian believers to do?

Paul continued his fatherly concern for the church in these verses. It was Israel's wisdom tradition for fathers to discipline their children. So Paul's request that the Corinthian believers imitate him was not a prideful comment on the heels of his teaching on humility. Instead, Paul was acknowledging that people learn from role models.

Who is looking up to you in faith? Write the name of two people who come to mind. (They might be children, grandchildren, nieces or nephews, neighbors, or people in your church or Bible study.)

1.

2.

Consider this question in a moment of quiet contemplation: Are you living in a way that will serve them well? Can you say, like Paul, "Watch my life and imitate me"?

Today we've explored God's message of "less talk, more action," and we've heard a strong emphasis on becoming a servant—someone who doesn't just say things about God but who lives out what she claims to believe. Paul emphasized this principle in our memory verse for this week, which happens to be one of my favorite verses.

Read and/or recite 1 Corinthians 4:20. In what ways does this verse convict and inspire you?

Digging Deeper

As we study the marks of maturity that Paul presented to help the Corinthian believers grow in faith, we might wonder how we can get "unstuck" and grow in our spiritual journeys. Check out the online Digging Deeper article for Week 2, "Unstuck," to explore some practial ways we can take next steps (see AbingdonPress.com /FirstCorinthians).

Let's close our study today by asking God to help us live lives of less talk, more action!

Talk with God

First, praise God that He never says, "Do as I say, not as I do." He sent His Son to live sacrificially, modeling for us the truths that He calls us to live—including how to live as a servant (under-rower) and a steward (overseer). Next, ask God to help you see any areas where your walk and talk might be out of alignment.

DAY 4: GOOD JUDGMENT

Yesterday in 1 Corinthians 4 we found Paul instructing the Corinthian believers not to judge their leaders or themselves because God alone is the master who renders judgment. Today in 1 Corinthians 5 we will find what, at first glance, looks like doublespeak as Paul passes judgment on a church member and asks the leaders to implement church discipline.

Paul knew the danger of Christians spending their time and energy criticizing one another rather than growing in Christ, but his words suggest that certain circumstances mandate judgment. So what is the difference between judging other believers and biblically addressing sin? How can we practice good judgment? This is what we will be exploring together today.

If we isolate some of Paul's statements in chapter 4, which we studied yesterday, it seems open and shut: we shouldn't judge. Period. But let's see what further insights we gain from chapter 5.

Read 1 Corinthians 5:1-8. What is Paul judging here?

Paul didn't ignore sin or bad behavior. In fact, all of Paul's letters, including this one written to the church in Corinth, contained judgments for individuals and the local church body with instructions—such as stop playing favorites among the leaders, avoid lawsuits with other believers, and quit being prideful. Paul seemed to make judgments a lot.

In reality, we all make judgments every day. We make judgments about whether to wear a particular outfit, eat the whole piece of cake, or verbalize a controversial thought. We need the Holy Spirit to guide us because the flesh likes to judge others with arrogance and self-righteousness, keeping us from looking at our own sin. So we must be careful and intentional about when and how we choose to judge.

Review verses 1-8 again, reading between the lines as you look for reasons why Paul felt it was necessary to judge in this instance.

A few things I notice that distinguish this situation from Paul's recommendations not to judge in the previous chapter include the following:

- The man's sin was clear (Leviticus 18:8), and it was habitual. This was not a judgment of motives or an issue of wisdom or preference.
- Rather than having an attitude of repentance, the man and the church boasted about the sin.
- The motivation for Paul's judgment was restoration of relationship to God and others, rather than self-righteous criticism or gossip.

Extra Insight

For the celebration of Passover, Jewish people remove all the items in their homes that contain leaven and eat bread without yeast for seven days, remembering how their ancestors left Egypt in such a hurry that they didn't have time to allow their bread to rise (see Deuteronomy 16:3-4).

- Paul called the leaders who had spiritual authority and personal relationship with the man to judge him.

Judgment is a tough subject for me. Paul's previous statements about letting God be the judge sit better with me. For a gal who errs on the side of grace rather than law, I need the Lord's help to understand how these words about judging, confronting, and even expelling a member of the church body are applicable in my life

The wide variety of churches and denominations that make up the body of Christ today coupled with a general attitude that sees church leaders as peers rather than authoritative overseers are two factors that complicate this concept of church discipline. Even to say that a sin is "clear" can be tough at times because we can have different interpretations of what is clear according to Scripture. And let's face it, sometimes even clear sin can seem to be muddy. In Scripture we find complexities such as God asking Abraham to sacrifice his son and Hebrew midwives lying to Pharaoh about the birth of their children in order to preserve the childrens' lives. Despite these challenges, striving to have a biblical understanding of sin is important if we are to practice good judgment. (For our purposes, I am using the term "clear sin" to mean those areas that Scripture refers to as an offense to God—such as lying, murder, adultery, and pride.)

Regrettably, when it comes to making judgments about others, too often we cast stones for things that are unclear in the Bible rather than clear, unrepentant, and habitual sins. What can help us as we attempt to apply God's unchanging Word in changing times?

When applying Scripture we must attempt to understand the culture of the original audience so that we can lift up and apply the unchanging principles against the backdrop of our modern culture. Many biblical principles do not need unwrapping, such as love your neighbor or forgive others or pray. However, other passages contain principles that come to life only as we gain a better understanding of the culture to which they were originally addressed.

Consider this illustration:

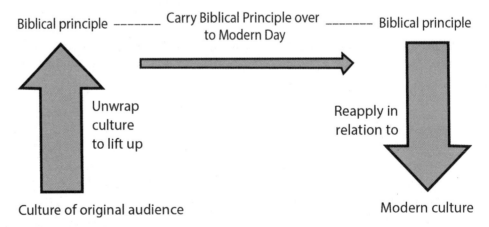

When it comes to applying Paul's instructions to the Corinthians, we would do well to look for the biblical principle here. Paul points out that there are times when church discipline becomes necessary for the good of all. Just as responsible parents do not ignore wrong behavior for the sake of their child, Paul knows that leaving this man in his sin will not only hurt the man but also influence the body as a whole. N. T. Wright uses medical terms to help us understand what Paul is saying:

> Is the doctor unloving or judgmental when he or she tells you that you must have the operation right away? Do we want a doctor who "tolerates" viruses, bacteria, cancer cells? And if we say that the moral issues Paul mentions in verse 11 are not like diseases, are we so sure? Do these things build up a community, or destroy it?[16]

Let's take this a step further and look at the specific sin Paul was addressing. Paul used the Greek word *porneia,* and in this context he was accusing this man of incest. As we learned earlier in our study, sexual sin was rampant in Corinth. However, incest was strictly forbidden under Roman law.[17] In two thousand years of church history, little has changed in this regard. Our culture also considers incest reprehensible—along with rape and child abuse—and rightly so; and sexual sin continues to be a problem, even in the church. Our culture takes a casual attitude about sexual morality but is outraged when Christian leaders preach faithfulness and then are discovered to be having affairs.

I've seen firsthand the devastating effects of sexual sin in the lives of Christians and the church:

- A dear friend was sexually abused as a child by a teacher at her Christian school.
- Another friend worked under a man who was soliciting prostitutes while masquerading as a faithful husband, father, and pastor.
- An extended family member receives the weekly web viewing history of several pastors who have asked for accountability in their efforts to turn from a pornography addiction.

Human nature hasn't changed. God hasn't changed. And though our culture is very different from that of Corinth, it is obsessed with sex just as Corinthian culture was. Paul teaches us to address sin because it affects so many others.

When sexual sin isn't addressed, what are some potential problems that can arise?

Perhaps you thought of future victims for a perpetrator or the stifling of growth in the lives of both the offender and those affected. Maybe you thought of the hypocrisy that the watching world trips over or the bad example set for new believers.

Read 1 Corinthians 5:6 in the margin. What illustration did Paul use for sin?

What is the role of yeast in the making of bread?

Now read Matthew 13:33 in the margin. What did Jesus say yeast does?

Not only does yeast permeate every part of the dough but it also is the ingredient that puffs it up. Wiersbe explains, "Leaven is a picture of sin. It is small but powerful; it works secretly; it 'puffs up' the dough; it spreads. The sinning church member in Corinth was like a piece of yeast; He was defiling the entire loaf of bread (the congregation)."[18]

Read Matthew 16:5-12 and summarize what Jesus was cautioning the disciples about:

Jesus told the disciples to look out for the deceptive teaching of the Pharisees. If Jesus judged anyone in his three years of ministry on this planet, it was the Pharisees. The Pharisees were Jewish religious leaders who taught strict adherence to the Law while often not following it themselves. They were known for their pride and desire for popularity, which is why they felt threatened by Jesus. They were missing the bigger picture of God's heart behind His laws.

Like Jesus' caution to the disciples, Paul calls us to stop overlooking blatant sin in the church. Grace divorced from truth can negatively impact the church body. We must learn to speak truth with grace. A good starting point is looking inward at our own sin. As we submit ourselves to the Lord in humility, we will maintain the right posture toward sin and keep ourselves from becoming stumbling blocks to other believers.

As we submit ourselves to the Lord in humility, we will maintain the right posture toward sin and keep ourselves from becoming stumbling blocks to other believers.

While you may not be struggling with sexual sin, we all battle sinful tendencies. Ask the Holy Spirit to bring to mind any clear, unrepentant, and habitual sin in your life. Are you boasting in something you know is wrong in the name of tolerance or freedom in Christ? Listen for anything the Lord reveals. Then write a short prayer below, asking the Lord to help you repent—to turn from your sin and turn to God.

Now read 1 Corinthians 5:2 in the margin. What does Paul say our posture toward sin in the church should be?

Paul says we should mourn over sin, rather than boast in how open-minded and tolerant we are.

Look up Galatians 6:1-2. What posture should we take when we help someone back on the right path? Circle three words in the attitude choices below:

gentle	prideful	humble	worried	insensitive
careful	quick	frequent	fearful	critical

God cares greatly about our attitude and posture when we address sin. When He puts us in a place of authority to correct another person, we should humbly, gently, and carefully confront that brother or sister with the goal being their repentance and restoration. Our response should be mourning rather than boasting when it comes to unrepentant, clear, and habitual sin committed by those in our own local body of believers.

Read 1 Corinthians 5:4-5. When addressing sin, what next steps should spiritual leaders take after mourning and assuming a humble and gentle posture?

You are so proud of yourselves, but you should be mourning in sorrow and shame. And you should remove this man from your fellowship. (1 Corinthians 5:2)

First, let's clear up the "hand him over to Satan" statement that sounds so harsh and difficult to swallow. The Bible sometimes refers to this world as a place where Satan has dominion (2 Corinthians 4:4; 1 John 5:19). Paul isn't talking about condemning the man but putting him back in the world that Satan controls outside the church. When talking about how to confront unrepentant believers, Jesus said the last phase of discipline is to treat them as a pagan or tax collector—in other words, those in the world (see Matthew 18:16-17). How did Jesus treat tax collectors and sinners? He called them to repentance and told them to sin no more, but He showed compassion as we see in the stories of Zacchaeus the tax collector and the woman caught in adultery.

Handing the man over to Satan meant allowing him to go back to the world, out of the church, until he came to his senses much like the prodigal son. Paul wanted the church at Corinth to take steps to confront sin, rather than ignore it, for the purpose of repentance and restoration. He knew it was more loving to take the cancer out than to ignore it and let it spread. One pastor and commentator put it this way: "Church discipline is not a group of 'pious policemen' out to catch a criminal. Rather, it is a group of brokenhearted brothers and sisters seeking to restore an erring member of the family."[19]

What new insights have you gained today about good judgment?

Tomorrow we will explore the next steps Paul gave the Corinthians to keep sin from being like yeast, permeating the church. Let's end today's lesson by summarizing how God calls us to deal with sin—whether our own or that of a brother or sister in Christ:

1. God calls us to mourn rather than boast about sin.
2. God asks spiritual leaders to humbly, gently, and carefully address unrepentant, habitual sin within the local church body.

Talking about sin isn't fun. But when we turn from our sin, we find grace and freedom on the other side and bring health and vitality to our souls and our communities of faith.

Talk with God

Spend some time praying for someone you know who is struggling with sin. Ask God to bring her or him to repentance. Then pray for the leaders in your church, asking the Lord to give them discernment, wisdom, and boldness to mourn over sin and address it as the Holy Spirit leads so that your local body of believers can grow toward greater maturity in faith.

DAY 5: RESTORATION

Lately I spend a lot of time sitting in stands. I watch one daughter beat on her drum in the marching band. Another chants, cheers, and jumps into the air to encourage the football players on the field. Still another runs much farther than I ever have in my life, competing in cross-country races. Watching my teenage children as a spectator, I see a lot of growth that has taken place since the stages of diapers, baby food, and potty-training. They have grown physically—my son towers over me and my twin daughters are over three inches taller than me. They also have matured emotionally, mentally, and spiritually (though the process certainly isn't over). Looking back, discipline definitely has played a role in their growth, along with encouragement, prayer, and many other factors.

This week we have seen that Paul spoke to the church at Corinth as a spiritual parent. He built them up, instructed them, and also gave them stern words of discipline when they veered off course.

Read 1 Corinthians 5:9-13 and answer the following questions:

Who should the church never judge? (v. 12)

Who will judge them? (v. 13)

Whom did Paul say the church is responsible to judge? (v. 12)

How did Paul say they should deal with those in the church who were sinning? (v. 13)

Now, we know that all of us are sinners and could be removed from the church if the only requirement was doing something wrong. So Paul must not have been talking about our everyday struggle with the flesh.

Look again at verses 10 and 11. What are some specific sins Paul named in both verses?

Extra Insight

The early church included fellowship meals as part of the celebration of the Lord's Supper, so when Paul calls the church not to eat with unrepentant sinners he likely was referring to Communion meals rather than eating together in general.

The Greek verbiage used here refers to those continuing in the habitual practice of these sins. These sins are clear and ongoing. When our kids were younger, we made a list of basement rules and posted them. No hitting. No throwing things. You get the idea. The basement was the place where they played unsupervised, so fights tended to break out often. We wanted the rules posted for clarity so my little lawyers wouldn't claim they forgot or didn't know the rules. Paul lists some of the practices that the people of Corinth indulged in that clearly were off limits for those who wanted to follow Christ. He didn't want them arguing over what he meant, so he repeated them.

Our attitude toward the sin in our lives is important. We can take different postures:

1. I'm struggling with sin but I desire to turn from it. I'm asking for help and accountability to turn from my sin and turn to God.
2. I'm going to practice this in my life no matter what God says about it. Even if technically it is sin according to the Bible, I know God will forgive me, and I'm not planning to change.

In your opinion, which of these two postures did the man Paul was referring to in chapter 5 seem to have taken toward his sin of immorality?

Paul wasn't empowering spiritual leaders to become fault-finders who oust people from the church for sport. Instead, he knew the need for church discipline in this man's life so that he might grow spiritually and so that the church family would not become infected with a relaxed attitude toward sin.

In Paul's second letter to the Corinthians, we find "the rest of the story" of what happened to the man Paul said they should remove from their fellowship.

Turn to 2 Corinthians 2:4-11 and answer the following questions.

What new instructions did Paul give the church in Corinth?

What additional insights do we gain here into Paul's attitude and motive for instructing them previously to remove the man?

Clearly Paul was brokenhearted over this situation (see verse 4). My husband, Sean, has been in similar situations as a pastor, and he says that those looking forward to confronting or reprimanding someone probably shouldn't do it. I wholeheartedly agree.

Now we don't know how this man reacted initially to correction, but according to what we read in 2 Corinthians 2, it seems that Paul believed he would welcome their forgiveness and restoration.

Take another look at 2 Corinthians 2:7-8. What does Paul encourage the church members and leaders to do? Check all that apply:

__ **Make him feel bad for all the trouble he caused.**

__ **Comfort him.**

__ **Continue to recount his sins behind his back.**

__ **Make assumptions about what he is thinking or feeling.**

__ **Affirm their love for him.**

__ **Forgive him.**

__ **Be on the lookout for Satan to try to accuse and blow up the situation again.**

__ **Continue to bring up his sins and talk about them.**

As parents, we know what this is like. After implementing consequences for our children's wrong behavior, we attempt to leave the situation in the past, affirm our love and forgiveness, comfort them if they must "eat the bitter fruit of living their own way" (Proverbs 1:31), and restore the relationship. Likewise, when our sisters and brothers in Christ are repentant, we are not to shame them but come alongside them in Christ, knowing we must constantly be on the lookout for our own sinful tendencies.

Paul wrote these things knowing our tendency to shoot our wounded, shifting attention to the public sinner in hopes that no one will discover our own battles with the flesh. Instead, Paul instructed the church to forgive, comfort, and be on the lookout for Satan to try to stir up disunity. This situation in Corinth reveals a milestone of growth for this man and for the body of Christ. Imagine the different ending to this story if the church had not intervened.

What have you learned about the positive benefits that can come from properly carrying out loving church discipline?

Like shepherds who watch over sheep, our spiritual leaders must care for the good of their entire flocks. Whether they are pastors, ministry leaders, deacons, elders, Sunday school teachers, or small group leaders, they will give an account to God for what they address and what they ignore.

Read Hebrews 13:17 in the margin. What is the responsibility of your spiritual leaders?

What are some practical ways we can give them reason to watch over us with joy instead of sorrow?

As we grow toward maturity in our faith, we learn that good judgment has restoration as its goal. Just as babies don't understand all that parents do to take care of them, sometimes we may not understand all that our spiritual leaders must do to care for us. But as we grow spiritually, we come to recognize that sometimes God calls them to intervene for the benefit of the church.

Talk with God

Talk with God about any questions you have about the principles we studied this week. Ask Him to reveal areas where He longs for you to grow toward greater maturity in regards to your relationships in the church. If you don't have a local church family, ask Christ to lead you to a church where you can forge deep relationships that will help you mature and practice some of the principles we learned this week about following Jesus in the context of community.

WEEKLY WRAP-UP

Note: This wrap-up exercise should take you approximately 6-7 minutes for reading the chapters and a few additional minutes for recording reflections.

Take a few minutes to read 1 Corinthians 3–5 again—either out loud if possible or silently if you are in a public setting. What new insights or applications did the Holy Spirit lift off the page as you read?

Here are some of the highlights from our study this week:

- Christ paid for our sins on the cross, and the only judgment we will face as believers will be a rewards judgment.
- We shouldn't judge the motives or intentions of others; only God can judge them correctly.
- Clear, unrepentant, habitual sin must be addressed by church leaders so that it will not harm the church community.
- Our response to sin should be mourning rather than boasting.
- The goal of church discipline should always be restoration.

How do these truths encourage and challenge your thinking about relationships within the church?

This week we've seen Paul's strong desire for the Corinthian believers to grow spiritually and progress toward maturity in faith. God also longs for us to have deeper roots as we pursue a close relationship with Him and others. He wants us to leave behind our spiritual bottles and baby food and cultivate a deeper walk with Him.

GROWING UP

I am not writing these things to shame you, but to _____ *you as my beloved*

_____.

(1 Corinthians 4:14)

Markers for Spiritual Growth

1. A progressing _____ _____

- Paul talked about our spiritual diet. (1 Corinthians 3:1-2)
- Baby – needs to be fed
- Child – needs to have food prepared but feeds self
- Teen/Young Adult – learns to prepare own food; self-sustaining
- Mature Believer – becomes a spiritual parent
- God's Word is our spiritual food. (Psalm 19:7-11)

2. Seeking to _____ _____ with others in imperfect churches
- Jealousy and quarrels reveal we are controlled by our sinful nature. (1 Corinthians 3:3)
- Letting the Spirit control us leads to life and peace. (Romans 8:6)

3. Building a life with _____ in mind
- We must build with good materials that will last into eternity. (1 Corinthians 3:10-16)

4. An attitude of _____
- Do not boast in a human leader. (1 Corinthians 3:21)
- Paul did not trust his own judgment in evaluating himself. (1 Corinthians 4:3)

VIDEO VIEWER GUIDE: WEEK 2

- Pride makes us forget our dependence on God. (1 Corinthians 4:8)
- We should mourn over sin and be teachable. (1 Corinthians 5:2)

5. Living by God's _____ rather than a lot of _____

- The Kingdom is not just talk but living by God's power. (1 Corinthians 4:20)
- God doesn't want us to be challenged but changed.

Week 3

EVERYBODY'S DOING IT

1 Corinthians 6–8

Memory Verse

But you must be careful so that your freedom does not cause others with a weaker conscience to stumble.

(1 Corinthians 8:9)

DAY 1: STANDING AGAINST INJUSTICE

Several years ago my friend's car was significantly damaged when winds blew her neighbor's fence across the yard and into her vehicle. The neighbor didn't feel it was his responsibility and wouldn't file a claim with his homeowner's insurance. Things became heated, and they ended up in small claims court. My friend won the case, but the relationship with her neighbor was ruined. Later they invited an elder from each of their respective churches to meet with them and try to work it out, but the effort came after the court had already made its decision. The car was repaired but the relationship remained strained until my friend moved a few years later.

In 1 Corinthians 6, we find Paul switching gears to talk about the matter of lawsuits in the church. Corinth was only forty-five miles from Athens where, according to Roman literature, lawsuits were prevalent and juries were as large as six hundred to one thousand people.[2] One commentator made this parallel between the two cities: "The legal situation in Corinth probably was much as it was in Athens, where litigation was a part of everyday life. It had become a form of challenge and even entertainment."[3] So here Paul is urging the Corinthian believers to stop acting like the world around them by engaging in hurtful lawsuits.

God calls us to live counterculture lives in the same way that Paul encouraged the Corinthian church to stop blending in with the surrounding culture. N. T. Wright offers this insight: "In the eyes of the world…a public dispute between Christians is a sign that Christians are really no different from everybody else. And 1 Corinthians is all about the fact that Christians *are* different from everybody else."[4] Unfortunately, so often what should be private disputes between believers become all too public, causing many to think that Christians today are no different than anyone else.

When it comes to lawsuits in our culture, we aren't too far from Corinth in our obsession with getting what we believe is owed to us. Check out these statistics:

- Over two hundred thousand civil suits were filed in the federal courts in one recent twelve-month period.
- Nearly one million lawyers (their number is increasing) are handling them.
- In one year, more than twelve million suits were filed in the state courts.[5]

In ancient Greek and Mediterranean culture, the legal system was a central part of everyday life. "Most common Hellenistic litigation involved property disputes."[1]

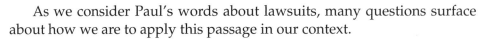

As we consider Paul's words about lawsuits, many questions surface about how we are to apply this passage in our context.

- How should we deal with disputes and lawsuits among Christians—especially when they attend different churches with different spiritual leaders?
- Do Paul's words about avoiding lawsuits apply to both criminal and civil cases?
- When is it appropriate to pursue justice in court?

These are some of the questions we will be exploring in our study today.

Turn to 1 Corinthians 6:1-8, our passage for today, and put a placeholder there. Read the verses and summarize one or two principles that stand out to you:

Paul began by saying, "When one of you has a dispute with another believer, how dare you file a lawsuit and ask a secular court to decide the matter instead of taking it to other believers!" (v. 1). Let's consider the precise meaning of the original language by looking to a commentator's insights:

> By "dare" (*tolma*), [Paul] strongly admonishes rather than commands Christians to take their legal grievances for set-tlement before qualified Christians. In this way, he allows for the possibility that under some circumstances Christians might take cases to the secular civil court.[6]

It is important to note that although Paul called the believers to avoid lawsuits, he did not say there was never a time to seek justice. We can infer that Paul's admonition referred to civil suits—as we will soon see—yet he was not forbidding all lawsuits involving property or assets, because sometimes in cases of divorce and in business dealings the law required the involvement of a secular court. Other instances such as theft, child abuse, or criminal activity were to be taken to the governing authorities as well. Paul certainly was not advocating that criminal activity should be handled by the church.

Look up Romans 13:1-5. What insights do these verses give us about God's view of a secular government's involvement in criminal affairs?

Now, turn back to 1 Corinthians 6:1-8. How does Paul intimate that he is referring to less significant incidents—civil suits? What words does he use to describe the kind of matters believers are disputing? (vv. 1-2)

What reasons does Paul give for why the church should feel equipped to judge these matters? (vv. 2-6)

What were the believers doing to one another through these lawsuits? (v. 8)

Though we don't know all the details of what was going on in the Corinthian church, we can glean three general truths from 1 Corinthians 6:1-8 that we can apply in our relationships with other believers—whether they involve lawsuits or not. Let's look briefly at each one.

1. Sacrificially love and care for one another.

Just because those in the world sue one another for sport and financial gain, we don't have to follow suit; we can love each other sacrificially instead. We can live counterculturally by focusing on relationships rather than rights. One way we can do this is choosing to forgive debts or damages in order to value people more than property.

> Think about the kinds of disputes we have with other believers over "ordinary matters." How can we work out our differences in a way that embraces community?

We can live counterculturally by focusing on relationships rather than rights.

Certainly one way we can apply Paul's words includes seeking to work things out ourselves for the benefit of all involved before running to unbelievers to settle the dispute for us.

2. Stand up against injustice.

Paul points out in verse 8 that through these lawsuits, believers were cheating one another. One source notes that "recent research on the court systems of the Roman empire has shown that…the overwhelming majority of civil cases were brought by the wealthy and powerful against people of lesser status and means."[7] So if believers were emulating the culture, it's possible that wealthy church members were engaging in lawsuits with lower-class members and swindling them. Paul didn't let this injustice slide but called it like he saw it!

Read Proverbs 31:8 in the margin. What does this verse instruct us to do?

When people are mistreated because of their economic level, race, age, gender, or any other reason, God calls us to speak up on their behalf. When we see true injustice, God asks us to open our mouths and defend those who need help defending themselves.

Many of our brothers and sisters in Christ face injustice or mistreatment—from those in our own backyards to those around the planet. Regardless of why they are being mistreated, they need our help.

What are some practical ways God might be calling you to stand up for injustice—whether across the globe, right in your own community, or anywhere in between?

God calls us to take a stand against injustice whenever we see people manipulated or cheated by others.

3. Be willing to take a loss.

Though we are always to stand up against the mistreatment of others, there are times when God asks us to be willing to take an undeserved hit ourselves. We need the Holy Spirit to help us identify those occasions. Ecclesiastes 3:1 says, "For everything there is a season, / a time for every activity under heaven." Two other statements in Ecclesiastes 3 relate to these types of justice situations:

- A time to scatter stones and a time to gather stones. (3:5)
- A time to be quiet and a time to speak. (3:7)

In verse 7 of today's passage, we see that Paul told the Corinthian believers their frivolous lawsuits were a defeat for them. He used the Greek legal word for *defeat*, insinuating that when believers sue each other, nobody wins.

My friend looks back and wonders what she should have done in the case of her damaged car. She had every right to be paid for the repairs, but was it worth the ruined relationship? By asking "Why not rather be wronged" (v. 7), Paul is saying the Corinthian believers could have chosen to accept an injustice. There is a time for everything: a time to fight for justice and a time to be willing to take a personal loss. We desperately need God's Holy Spirit to guide us and give us supernatural wisdom to navigate these often tenuous situations.

We also can look to the teachings of Jesus for help. Jesus instructed us to be willing to endure unjust treatment at times.

Read Matthew 5:39-41 in the margin, and fill in the chart below:

Verse	When someone:	You should:
39	Slaps you on the right cheek	
40	Sues you in court and your shirt is taken	
41	Demands you carry his gear for a mile	

39 "But I say, do not resist an evil person! If someone slaps you on the right cheek, offer the other cheek also. 40 If you are sued in court and your shirt is taken from you, give your coat, too. 41 If a soldier demands that you carry his gear for a mile, carry it two miles." (Matthew 5:39-41)

How do these verses support our third principle about being willing to take a loss?

Consider a conflict you might be involved in right now—with a family member, church member, coworker, neighbor, or friend. How might Jesus be calling you to follow Him by giving up your rights?

We must be sure we aren't on the wrong end of justice. Though we should never be the ones who treat others unfairly, at times we must accept unfair treatment. This isn't easy, but it is necessary for the body of Christ to function in its mission of reaching the lost. As we reflect on today's passage, the question we must ask ourselves is, "How we can we best love other believers and glorify God in our decisions?"

Remember that this passage doesn't say we should never go to court. Instead, it tells us to avoid lawsuits; and if we can't escape courtrooms

based on our circumstances, we should seek God's glory rather than our own material gain. Our need to be dependent on God through the power of His Spirit will be critical to us in those times.

While some of the passages we are studying from Paul's letter may be difficult to apply directly in our lives, they help us grow a bigger view of God in our hearts and minds, which trickles into our thoughts, attitudes, and behaviors.

Take a moment to rewrite in your own words the three principles from today's passage:

1.

2.

3.

Based on these principles, is God calling you to take any steps or make any changes in your relationships? If so, what are they?

Talk with God

Prayerfully read 1 John 3:14-18, and ask God to give you His sacrificial love for the other believers He has placed in your life. In the margin, write the names of a few believers God is calling you to love with your actions, and spend a few moments praying for each one by name.

DAY 2: SEX

For years I didn't like to say the title of today's lesson out loud. Don't laugh at me. I grew up in the rural South where the word *fart* mentioned aloud made us blush. I remember as a fourth-grader someone asking me if I knew what "it" meant. I played along but had no idea they were referring to sex. Even those who were talking about it as kids didn't want to say the word aloud. Marrying a Canadian and living north of the Mason-Dixon Line for a few decades has loosened me up, but I'm still not as open and free as my husband and many of my girlfriends are in talking about this subject. So if you aren't anxious to delve into this topic today, know that I am with you. Yet we need to push past our comfort level and hear what God has to say. If He included it in the Bible, then it's important.

In today's passage we will find that Paul spoke openly about sex. He didn't shy away from personal topics—especially when they related to the

Corinthian believers' tendency to be influenced by the world around them. In a city where sexual sin was normalized, Paul called them to realign with God's truth and look for areas where their former worldly habits were slowly seeping back into their lives.

My prayer is that we will do the same. As we study, let's ask God to bring to light any areas where the influence of the world around us might be causing us to compromise. And let's remember to look for God's heart of protection in Paul's sometimes harsh-sounding fatherly words.

Read our passage for today, 1 Corinthians 6:9-20, and put a placeholder there. What do we learn about the past lives of some of the Corinthian believers from verses 9-11? Rather than list all the sins mentioned, how would you summarize their lives?

Paul originally preached in the Jewish synagogue, but very few Jews received his message. So he went to the Gentiles with the message of Christ. Like Jesus, Paul spent time with sinners, sharing the possibility of a new life in Christ for broken and hurting people.

According to verse 11, what made the change in their lives?

Now think for a minute about your life before Christ. Whether you decided to follow Him as a small child, a teenager, or an adult, He cleansed you from all your sins and made you holy through His shed blood. We all have old habits and sins from our pasts that we continue to battle. Coming to Christ doesn't end the struggle with sin, but it does give us power through God's Spirit to overcome old tendencies that used to enslave us.

How have you seen God free you from personal sin patterns that you have battled?

Your past or present struggle may not be found among the sins listed in verses 9-10, but those were the ones the Corinthians were battling. The truth is that all of us struggle with sinful thoughts, attitudes, and actions. (Selfishness and pride rear their ugly heads in my life continually.) Paul addresses our need to remember God's call to holiness so we won't fall back into old habits that the culture around us still engages in.

Extra Insight

"Many Jewish men in Paul's day were under pressure to pretend they were Gentiles, and some even tried surgery to make it look as though they were uncircumcised after all (Greeks went naked when they took exercise, or used public baths, so Jewish identity was all too obvious)."[8]

According to verses 12-13, what two excuses were the believers making? (Look for a statement in each verse.)

1.

2.

Let's look at each of these excuses for continuing in sin used by the Corinthian believers. The first excuse was, "I am allowed to do anything." The message of Christ had liberated Jews from strict adherence to the law, bringing newfound freedom in Christ. Yet apparently this freedom had become an excuse for license for many in the Corinthian church.

How did Paul respond to their statement of liberty used as an excuse for license? (v. 12)

God knows our tendency to trade our freedom for a new kind of slavery.

Summarize the following verses in your own words:

Galatians 5:13

Romans 6:1-4

How do these passages connect with what Paul is teaching in 1 Corinthians 6 about not using our freedom in Christ as an excuse to sin?

> We are free in Christ, but God wants us to use our freedom to overcome sin, not become enslaved to it.

We are free in Christ, but God wants us to use our freedom to overcome sin, not become enslaved to it. As Romans 6:4 says, "For we died and were buried with Christ by baptism. And just as Christ was raised from the dead by the glorious power of the Father, now we also may live new lives." It broke Paul's heart as a spiritual father to watch the Corinthians use their freedom in Christ as an excuse to continue in sins that would harm them spiritually.

Let's bring this closer to home. Spend a moment evaluating your struggle with sin. None of us is free from needing to confess regularly the areas where we battle sin. Whether we struggle with selfishness, worldly behavior, addiction, unkindness, or some other sin, God's grace, patience, and love should motivate us to turn from our sin—not engage more freely in it.

If a "spiritual parent" (mentor or leader) was writing you a letter to address where you are making excuses for sin in your life, what topics do you think would be included? (Just write the first letter of the word or words that come to mind if you want.)

Present these struggles to the Lord now. He already knows them. Express your desire to turn from your sin and toward God's freedom—rather than be enslaved to old habits. If you like, write your prayer in the margin.

A moment ago we read in Romans 6:1-4 that we have died to sin and been raised with Christ to live new lives. The rest of Romans 6 assures us that the same power that raised Jesus from the dead is available to help us do just that. Through Christ, we are free to obey, not continue in sin!

The second excuse the believers in Corinth used to support their sexual sin was the comment "Food was made for the stomach, and the stomach for food." To understand this comment, we must realize that during this time a group of teachers alleged that body and spirit were completely separate entities. One commentator explained it this way: "Much Greek philosophy considered everything physical, including the body, to be basically evil and therefore of no value. What was done with or to the body did not matter. Food was food, the stomach was the stomach, and sex was sex. Sex was just a biological function like eating, to be used just as food was used, to satisfy their appetites."[9]

Once again worldly philosophy had spilled over into the believers' thinking. Paul drew them back to the truth of God's Word, reminding them that God cares about our bodies.

Reread 1 Corinthians 6:15-17 and summarize Paul's arguments:

Based on these thoughts, Paul initiated two clear directives in verses 18-20. Write them in the chart on the next page:

Verse	Directive
18	
20	

What reason does Paul give to run from sexual sin? (v. 18)

We know that all sin offends our holy God. Paul doesn't say that sexual sin is worse than any other sin. The Father sent His only Son to die for every sin, and we can't make a chart of the level or degree of each sin. *All* sin separates us from God. However, we read in the Bible how sexual sin led to great struggles and significant consequences—even for

- the strongest of people (Samson),
- the wisest of individuals (Solomon),
- and the most devoted to God (David).

If these great servants of God could fall to sexual temptation, we should not think ourselves immune to the possibility. As Paul pointed out, sexual sin carries with it consequences we should consider seriously as followers of Christ. His words are a yellow light of caution, warning that sexual sin

- harms those involved—both emotionally and physically.
- gains control over people, becoming addictive.
- perverts God's purpose for our bodies, which were made to honor God and be indwelt by the Holy Spirit.

The Lord longs for us to see ourselves the way He does: holy. Paul used the Temple as an illustration of what our bodies become when we invite Christ to take up residence within us. Jesus paid the ultimate price to redeem us from slavery, so Paul reminded the Corinthian believers to use their bodies to honor God instead of indulge their flesh.

When it comes to sexuality, we can relate to the Corinthians, who allowed worldly thinking to creep back into their lives. Social media, television, radio, movies, and the Internet give us so many opportunities for temptation. While we may want to say that guys struggle with sexual sin more than us gals, we certainly are not immune to the battle.

Our struggles may be different. God may call some of us to stop reading trashy novels or watching sexually explicit television shows or movies, some of us to stay off certain Internet sites, and others of us to stop flirting with a coworker. Only we know the secret sin issues of our own hearts. Regardless of our areas of weakness, God calls all of us to run from sexual sin and honor Him with our bodies.

Write two principles or insights that have stood out to you from today's lesson.

1.

2.

God's heart is *for* us. He longs to free us from the sin that so easily entangles us, and He has given us the power of His Spirit so that we can turn from sin and toward Him, remembering that Jesus bought us with a high price (1 Corinthians 6:20). I love the way one author reflects on today's passage. It's a fitting conclusion for our study today:

> If you pay a lot of money for a wonderful book, you don't start tearing pages out to make shopping lists, or writing rude words in the margins. If you pay a lot of money for a lovely house, you don't spray-paint silly patterns on the front door. In the same way, those who have been "bought" at tremendous cost must remind themselves of what special people they are, and learn to behave accordingly.[10]

You weren't cheap, my friend, so treat yourself like you would your most prized possession!

Talk with God

Thank God for the body He has given you. While you await your perfect body in heaven, take a few minutes to marvel at the many intricate systems and parts of your body that enable you to see, process information, walk, and function. Ask God to reveal any changes you can make to honor Christ more completely with your body. Then seek His guidance and help to make changes that will set you free.

DAY 3: PREFERENCES AND ABSOLUTES

I remember sitting in class over twenty years ago and hearing my favorite Bible professor respond to a question by explaining his position on a finer point of theology. He ended by saying, "But I wouldn't burn for that one." We all laughed, but he went on to explain the importance of knowing what you are so sure of that you would be willing to "burn at the stake" before recanting.

The longer I study the Bible, the shorter my list of "certainties" becomes. It includes—but certainly is not limited to—things such as

- God's great love for humanity,
- sin's ability to separate us from God,

Jesus bought us with a high price.... You weren't cheap, my friend, so treat yourself like you would your most prized possession!

- the cross of Christ being the payment for sin,
- the need for a personal relationship with God through Christ,
- and God's Word being alive and active.

For these things I would give my life if asked to recant. On many other topics I have strong opinions but acknowledge that I might be wrong. Over my years of life, study, and learning, I have changed my mind regarding my stance in certain areas of spiritual life and practice. Things I once spent a lot of time contemplating, I now see in a different light. Other things that I glossed over in my early years I now see as having great importance. I read, study, and seek answers as I attempt to interpret and apply God's Word in my life. For some things I would be willing to burn at the stake; for others I could say, "I wouldn't burn for that one."

Today we are studying 1 Corinthians 7, in which Paul gives instructions on marriage; but our focus will be on the idea that some things are preference issues whereas others are absolutes. Paul sometimes gives his best advice while reminding the Corinthians that it won't be a sin if they don't take it. Warren Wiersbe recommends we keep in mind that "Paul is replying to definite questions. He is not spelling out a complete 'theology of marriage' in one chapter."[11] The things Paul addresses here are not "burn at the stake" issues; they are judgment calls and wisdom issues that helped the church at Corinth. We'll discover that just as Jesus feasted and John the Baptist fasted, God may have different directions for people in various seasons of life and ministry.

As you read today's chapter, keep these helpful thoughts in mind:

- The church wrote to Paul asking for advice on these matters (this isn't unsolicited instruction).
- Paul was their spiritual father (he had authority to give instruction).
- This chapter is included in God's inspired Word, which is alive, active, and relevant to us today.

Read 1 Corinthians 7:1-24, and circle the correct letter to complete each statement below:

1. **Paul says the only reason a husband and wife should abstain from sexual intimacy for a limited time is:**

   a. headache

   b. prayer

   c. fatigue

> **Just as Jesus feasted and John the Baptist fasted, God may have different directions for people in various seasons of life and ministry.**

2. Paul wishes everyone was single but recognizes that it's better to marry than burn with:

   a. loneliness

   b. longing

   c. lust

3. In discussing whether a believer should stay with an unbelieving spouse, Paul says to:

   a. make the unbelieving spouse stay even if he or she wants to leave

   b. pursue living in peace with an unbelieving spouse

   c. leave an unbelieving spouse to try to find a better one

4. As people come to know Christ in Corinth, Paul says they should:

   a. not try to change their circumstances but follow Christ in their present situations

   b. remember the important thing is to obey God's commandments rather than change their jobs or human traditions

   c. both a and b

As we look for modern applications to the issues facing the Corinthian church, we find Paul, their spiritual leader, sometimes answering with a direct command from the Lord and other times stating he doesn't have one. Paul makes it clear what constitutes an absolute and which issues are instructions that relate to specific individuals.

When it comes to God's plans for our lives, we find two different kinds of instructions.

1. God's prescriptive will. These things are God's will for everyone in every culture in every generation. Some examples would be:

- Love your neighbor.
- Pray.
- Forgive.

Our gracious Lord doesn't leave us to wonder in these and many other areas. Throughout His Word, He lets us know His prescriptive will for us, His people.

Extra Insight

"Paul did not learn his views of marriage from the Jewish environment in which he had been brought up. There marriage was regarded as obligatory for men."[12]

What are some commands from Scripture that you would categorize as prescriptive—instructions that are true for every believer?

2. God's permissive will. Other times things aren't so straightforward. These are the times when we find in God's Word different instructions for different people. Today's passage is a great example. In Scripture we see that God has different decisions in mind for different people related to topics such as marriage or singleness (1 Corinthians 7), food choices (Romans 14), and trials (Hebrews 11:32-38). Other areas where God may lead us to make different decisions include how we educate our children, what health and medical options we choose, and whether we work outside the home. Within God's permissive will, He may lead us to follow Him in opposite ways through the leading of the Holy Spirit. Yet sometimes we think God's leading for us must be right for everyone.

What are some issues about which you have made decisions according to God's permissive will? These are things that are right for you but may not be right for others.

Can you think of times you have felt shamed or judged by another believer for your choices? Describe an incident that comes to mind:

> We wouldn't need a relationship with God or the guidance of the Holy Spirit if a specific answer for every decision . . . was to be found in the pages of the Bible.

In today's passage we find a good reminder that God doesn't give a prescriptive command for every area of life. We wouldn't need a relationship with God or the guidance of the Holy Spirit if a specific answer for every decision we will ever make was to be found in the pages of the Bible. God's Word is alive and gives us guidance and help, but it should lead us to a deeper relationship with Jesus—not replace that relationship with an exhaustive list of do's and don'ts. That kind of legalistic living is more consistent with the Pharisees than the disciples.

Now read 1 Corinthians 7:25-40, looking for examples of both God's prescriptive will and His permissive will. Then label each of the following statements either PRES for prescriptive or PERM for permissive. Here's a guideline to help you:

Prescriptive will: The same for all people.

Permissive will: Not the same for all people.

_____ 1. It is best for young women to remain single because of the present crisis.

_____ 2. A young woman can marry but will have troubles.

_____ 3. Those who use the things of this world should not become attached to them.

_____ 4. I want you to do whatever will help you serve the Lord best, with as few distractions as possible.

_____ 5. A man who thinks he will give in to his passion with his fiancée can marry her.

_____ 6. A man who can control his passion does well not to marry.

As I read Paul's words, only numbers three and four seem prescriptive to me. These principles apply universally to all believers in any situation. The other commands refer to what is right for each individual *according to her or his personal struggles and circumstances.*

Understanding the difference in God's prescriptive and permissive will is critical as we interact as a community of believers. The dangers of projecting God's permissive will for us individually as absolutes for other believers can be devastating. We can be tempted to judge, gossip, or speak harshly to others who need our encouragement rather than our condemnation in their journey of faith.

I once heard a story of two close friends who had served together for many years. Typically the two friends carried a lot on their plates and encouraged each other as they pursued Jesus in the same church and school system. But then one of the gals felt called to a season of rest. Her family had begun providing foster care and felt the need to simplify their lives, so she stepped down from several church, community, and school responsibilities. These changes interrupted the regular flow of the women's friendship in a few ways.

The woman who had been called to rest began to see great benefits for her family and faith, and she wondered why her friend continued to do all the things they had done before. However, her friend wasn't called to foster care and didn't sense God leading her to back away from teaching Sunday school, helping with youth group, and making meals for people. The friends discussed the changes and found they both resented each other a little. The gal called to rest didn't understand why her friend didn't

want to take a break since it was so needed in her own life. The woman continuing to serve felt the burden of the holes that were created by her friend's absence.

It isn't always easy to recognize and encourage those who are called to different things than we are. Our fleshly tendency is judgment when someone follows God in a different direction than ours. First Corinthians teaches us that although God never asks us to compromise sound doctrine, He may call us down different paths in life and ministry.

End your study today by taking a few moments to consider where you need to realign with God's grace toward others who think differently than you. Ask the Lord to give you a discerning mind to see the difference between preferences and absolutes in your life and community of faith.

Talk with God

Spend some time in prayer reflecting on the truths for which you would burn at the stake. Ask God to help you never compromise when it comes to His gospel message. Then seek God's direction to see where you are following His permissive will that might be different from those around you. Pray for eyes of grace and understanding to cheer on your sisters and brothers in Christ rather than expecting them to think and live just as you do.

Extra Insight

"Meats which had been sacrificed in the temple were used at all social festivities."[13]

DAY 4: INFORMATION OVERLOAD

Sometimes I wonder how I ever functioned as a human being before online search engines. How did I ever get to the right place without the map app on my phone telling me when to turn right and left? Did I really go to the doctor every time I had a question about swimmer's ear or bee stings instead of using online medical sites? Many times when my teenagers ask me something, I advise them to Google it. This word wasn't in my vocabulary as a child. My kids can't believe the world still spun before cell phones, laptops, and Wi-Fi.

However, the down side to all this knowledge at our fingertips is information overload—and unnecessary guilt. Years ago we didn't have guilt because our kids' birthday party favors weren't up to par to those on Pinterest or because we found out that we paid more for the same shoes we could have bought online.

Occasionally, ignorance is bliss. On days when I scroll through social media too long, I feel my brain about to burst with everything from a friend's sick dog to all the birthdays of extended family members to a stranger's unbelievable medical challenges. Perhaps knowing so much about everybody has some downsides, too.

In what ways have you experienced information overload?

Knowledge can make us feel important, but we'll find today in 1 Corinthians 8 that it had some downsides for the Corinthians as well. Knowledge was greatly valued and almost worshiped by the people of Corinth. While they didn't have Google or Siri, they did spend time discussing all different philosophies of life. As a port city, they had people from around the world pass through their city espousing all different sorts of ideas. Paul wanted to help the Corinthian church members see that epistemology—the study of knowledge—wasn't the only factor to use in decision-making as a follower of Jesus.

In 1 Corinthians 8, the issue facing the church at Corinth that we read about had to do with meat sacrificed to idols. Since there's not a "meat-sacrificed-to-idols" section in our grocery stores, we need to gain a greater understanding of how this issue played out in daily Corinthian life.

First of all, this was a topic difficult to avoid. Food wasn't just nourishment for the Corinthians; it was social. Greek culture hasn't changed much in regards to a love for family gatherings, entertaining, and food shopping. I have a Greek friend who often tells me about their celebrations and special foods when they gather with extended family. Greeks don't just have big fat Greek weddings; they have big fat Greek parties for most holidays and special occasions.

Greek temples in that time were social gathering places similar to a banquet hall. This was where people gathered for big family dinners, parties, or even business gatherings. People brought animals to sacrifice, and the priests would offer them to the god or goddess of that temple. Then some of the meat would be cooked and prepared for the people who had brought the animal. Almost always more meat was left over than could be eaten, so the rest was taken to the markets and sold. Most of the meat available for sale in a city such as Corinth had been previously sacrificed to a local god or goddess.

So the Corinthian Christians faced some difficult decisions. Should they eat meat in the temple if they were invited to a family gathering or business meeting? Should they purchase meat from local markets, knowing it likely had been butchered in a temple and offered as a sacrifice to an idol or fake god? The Corinthians had asked Paul what they should do on this issue. Rather than answer them directly, Paul helped them understand how to navigate issues of conscience.

Read Paul's response in 1 Corinthians 8:1-8, putting a placeholder there. Then respond to the questions on the following page:

Extra Insight

An issue of conscience is a gray area not clearly forbidden or allowed according to the Bible. We each must make individual decisions according to God's personal leading in our lives on issues that are not black and white.

What does Paul say a potential pitfall of knowledge can be? (v. 1)

How is love superior to knowledge? (v. 1)

Complete this chart according to verses 2 and 3:

The person who:	Is the one who:
Claims to know all the answers	
Loves God	

After reading verses 1-3, how would you summarize the content of these verses to a friend?

Like the Corinthians, we live in a culture where knowledge is considered power. How do these verses encourage or convict you personally?

Reading about humility and love trumping knowledge makes me want to shout these truths from a mountaintop. The power of these truths both lifts the weight of having to know it all and, at the same time, convicts me of my tendency to want to be right rather than to respond in love. I like to know the right answer. (Is anyone with me?) But God is showing us here that in some cases where we apply principles differently according to our various backgrounds, sin issues, personalities, or traditions, there is no one-size-fits-all principle to apply. What is right for one believer might be wrong for another.

We can't rely solely on logic and facts but, instead, must make decisions based on love. The Bible tells us that "God is love" (1 John 4:8). Through a vibrant relationship with God, we can discern the most loving thing to do in every situation. He calls us to live love even when we disagree—perhaps especially when we disagree. Bible teacher Ray Stedman says it this way:

> Love involves a willingness to get inside another person's skin, another person's viewpoint, and see the world through that person's eyes. Knowledge is self-centered: "I know such-and-such is true." Love is focused on others: "Because of my love for you, I want to know what you are thinking, what you are feeling, what you know to be true, what you need and want and desire." Love builds others up.[14]

Look again at 1 Corinthians 8:4-8. What was the issue that divided the Corinthian Christians according to these verses?

Through a vibrant relationship with God, we can discern the most loving thing to do in every situation.

On one side of the fence we have the believers who have no problem eating meat sacrificed to an idol because they know idols are nonsense. The argument of the Corinthians who had a good grasp of the ridiculousness of idols was that they felt free to eat meat no matter where it was slaughtered. Perhaps they were familiar with Peter's vision recorded in Acts 10, when God told Peter that no food was unclean if God said it was clean. They had logic, knowledge, and examples to make a good argument for the freedom to eat meat no matter where it had been butchered.

However, on the other side of the issue were those who formerly had worshiped idols—or even served as temple prostitutes (we read about these believers in 1 Corinthians 6:9-11, which we studied on Day 2). Eating meat that had been sacrificed to gods they had formerly worshiped left them unsettled in their conscience.

All of us can admit that our past impacts our present. Our experiences can grow us in wisdom, but they also can make us extra-sensitive in certain areas. As we uncover the roots beneath our sensitivities, we can prayerfully evaluate whether God is calling us to avoid temptation or grow in freedom.

Paul says in chapter 8 that we know food is food. In verse 8 he admits, "It's true that we can't win God's approval by what we eat. We don't lose anything if we don't eat it, and we don't win anything if we do." These are the cold, hard facts of the situation. Yet God wants us to understand that life isn't always just about facts. Our questions must go beyond "What are the facts?" to "Based on the facts, background, and human tendencies, what is most loving in this situation?"

Though we do not face the specific issue of whether or not to eat meat sacrificed to idols, that doesn't mean these chapters are irrelevant to us. We too struggle to rightly apply knowledge and love to issues of conscience.

What comes to mind when you think of areas where we disagree about how to apply our freedom in Christ? Consider choices or decisions that might be acceptable for one person but considered to be sin for another in light of her or his past.

A few that came to mind for me include:

- School choices for our kids (a child's personality, struggles, and parental resources can be factors)
- Views on alcohol (a family history of addiction, cultural acceptability, and a history of moderation are variables)
- Media choices (age appropriateness, violent or sexual content, and the worldview espoused can influence choices)

We all face decisions of conscience where we must decide God's leading for us personally while realizing He may lead others differently. When we start to think we have all the answers, we need to remember that we really don't know very much. Rather than thinking we are always right and those who disagree with us are always wrong, we must realize that sometimes in matters of conscience others are simply different. As Paul reminds us, truth and love must go hand in hand as we seek to love God wholeheartedly and discern His will in our lives.

How do you discern between biblical truth that should not be compromised and issues of conscience?

Today's passage helps us remember that some topics, such as the gospel message, are foundational—true for every believer everywhere—while others are areas of liberty that must be approached with a looser grip, realizing that one size doesn't fit all.

Think of a conscience issue where you disagree with another believer. How do your thoughts, words, and actions related to this issue reflect love?

Do you ever find yourself making puffed up, smug remarks? Do you look down on those who disagree with you as inferior to your

> **Rather than thinking we are always right and those who disagree with us are always wrong, we must realize that sometimes in matters of conscience others are simply different.**

views? If you answered yes to either question, what are some ways that you can disagree better?

As we close today, let's review some principles from today's passage that can help us reimagine those with whom we disagree as co-heirs of God's grace:

- Knowledge makes us feel important, but love strengthens the church.
- Anyone who thinks she (or he) knows all the answers really doesn't know very much.
- The person who loves God is the one whom God recognizes.
- There is only one God who created all things and through whom we live.
- Our previous lives of sin can weaken our consciences, so that we need to refrain from activities in which other Christians are free to engage.
- What is right for us might be wrong for another believer.

Tomorrow we will finish chapter 8, emphasizing our need to consider others when implementing decisions of conscience. We'll find that in light of all we studied today, God may call us to limit our own freedoms for the sake of others.

Talk with God

Address your own information overload today by laying aside all other thoughts and worries and meditating on one thing: God's great love for you. You can't live love toward others apart from Him. Slowly read and embrace the thoughts expressed in 1 John 4:7-12.

DAY 5: LIBERTY AND LOVE

My high school friend grew up in a home where alcohol was abused by both of her parents. As a little girl, she watched them fight under the influence of liquor. She remembers one particular night when she ran through a field to a neighbor's house to call the police because her father had a gun pointed at her mother, and she was scared. Her dad's multiple offenses for driving under the influence eventually landed him in jail.

When my friend came to know Christ in high school, she began a wholehearted pursuit of a new life. She steered clear of alcohol completely during her high school, college, and early-married years; she couldn't even be around it. Today she has friends who feel differently about alcohol than she does and who occasionally have alcoholic drinks in moderation, but she

> Truth and love must go hand in hand as we seek to love God wholeheartedly and discern His will in our lives.

Extra Insight

"The word *conscience* simply means 'to know with,' and it is used thirty-two times in the New Testament. Conscience is that internal court where our actions are judged and are either approved or condemned (Rom. 2:14-15)."[15]

> We have a tendency to judge another's weakness or sensitivity in an area where we are strong.

doesn't judge them. They agree on Ephesians 5:18, which instructs us not to get drunk but to be filled with the Spirit. Still, she chooses not to drink because she knows that she comes from a family of addictive personalities, and she has seen too much devastation to take a chance that she might struggle with moderation herself.

How is this scenario somewhat similar to the issue of meat sacrificed to idols that we studied yesterday?

As we finish 1 Corinthians 8 today, we will find that we must not make decisions based on ourselves alone. God calls us to think of others when it comes to living out our Christian freedoms. What is safe for one person could be quite unsafe for another. We have a tendency to judge another's weakness or sensitivity in an area where we are strong. Through the Apostle Paul, God teaches us that our posture should be to help, not judge, those whose conscience issues differ from ours. In fact, we should be willing to sacrifice our freedoms in order to strengthen others.

At times I wonder why certain Scriptures can seem vague or confusing. All Scripture is equally true, but it is not all equally clear. Some instructions in the Bible can lead us to think one thing, while another passage seems to lend itself to an opposite viewpoint. We can see why the Corinthian Christians were asking Paul about meat sacrificed to idols. When Gentiles first joined the Jewish Christians in faith, much dialogue occurred as to which laws should be applied.

Read Acts 15:28-29 in the margin. Record below what was included in the few restrictions the apostolic council decreed for new Gentile converts:

28 "For it seemed good to the Holy Spirit and to us to lay no greater burden on you than these few requirements: 29 You must abstain from eating food offered to idols, from consuming blood or the meat of strangled animals, and from sexual immorality. If you do this, you will do well. Farewell." (Acts 15:28-29)

Paul could have pointed to this as absolute proof that meat sacrificed to idols should be prohibited. However, he did not pronounce a clear-cut answer to their question. Instead, he wanted to teach them to wrestle and pray through questions, considering the implications for individuals, the faith community, and the watching world. Having a balance of Christ-centered knowledge and love as the foundation of the church resonates today as we seek to work through our own hot-button issues—such as spiritual gifts, the roles of men and women, alcohol, and guns, to name a few.

My husband, Sean, and his good friend are like-minded in much regarding faith, family, and even politics, but they tread carefully when they speak about guns because they hold diametrically opposing views on this topic. The enemy would love to take one small area where opinions differ and use it to separate an encouraging relationship. Thankfully, these two men have chosen to realize that their common ground far outweighs their differences. Unfortunately, I've seen other relationships torn apart over opposing viewpoints.

How have you seen relationships among believers affected by a disagreement over a gray area or conscience issue?

The enemy would love to take one small area where opinions differ and use it to separate an encouraging relationship.

Many times our disagreements involve things that aren't even mentioned in the Bible. I love this story of two amazing men of God from church history:

> Two of the most famous preachers in nineteenth-century England were Charles Haddon Spurgeon and Joseph Parker. They were close friends who sometimes held evangelistic meetings together. But they also had disagreements. On one occasion, Spurgeon learned that Parker had attended the theater in London. Spurgeon confronted his friend and said, "A truly spiritual Christian knows that it's worldly to attend the theater."
>
> Parker chuckled. "Tell me Charles—what's that hanging out of your mouth?"
>
> Spurgeon puffed on his cigar, "Surely, you don't suggest there's anything wrong with having a smoke?"
>
> Parker said, "Many Christians would say that a truly spiritual Christian should know that it's worldly to go around smoking like a chimney!"
>
> Both men eventually agreed that there was not a word in the Bible against either the theater or a good cigar and that they would have to tolerate each other's Christian liberty in these gray areas of life.[16]

In the midst of our own gray areas, God wants us to study and seek truth but also consider how it will impact our unity.

Read 1 Corinthians 8:9-13 and complete the following sentences using your own words (answers may vary according to translations):

Be careful so that_____

_____. (v. 9)

If others see you eating in the temple of an idol, _____

_____. (v. 10)

Your knowledge could cause _____. (v. 11)

Encouraging other believers to violate their conscience is actually sinning against _____. (v. 12)

I don't want to cause another believer to _____. (v. 13)

Paul warned that the weaker brother or sister watching a mature believer exercise freedom to eat meat might be destroyed. Frank Gaebelein helps us clarify what is meant by the word *destroyed* (or *ruined*) in verse 11: "Paul does not mean ultimate spiritual destruction, for he calls this man a 'brother, for whom Christ died.' The stress is on weakening the faith and ruining the Christian life of the brother [or sister]."[17]

When we feel free to engage in behavior that is controversial to other Christians, we must consider that they may have a different conviction than we hold, a background that limits their freedom in this area, or sin tendencies pertaining to this liberty (while our sin tendencies prohibit us in other areas). For example, I've seen Christian women divide over issues such as whether to watch a particular reality TV show together, allow their children to watch certain movies or TV channels, permit their kids to attend school dances, or wear a bikini.

What can you add to this list?

Paul asks us to consider if exercising our freedom might hinder a weaker—or more sensitive—brother or sister in Christ.

An example in my own life relates to allowing kids to dress up for Halloween. Sean and I allow our children to collect candy and enjoy time with our neighbors (I will say more about that in Week 4). However, I have an extended family member who views the subject very differently. If her family happens to be visiting us at the end of October, we will make alternate plans and possibly go out to dinner on that night. We hold to our liberties but put others' convictions above our rights.

Now, we need a caution light here as we observe how this passage has been applied out of context among modern believers. This portion of Paul's letter was not intended to hold an entire church hostage to the whims of the most legalistic member. Richard Hays notes that "the 'stumbling block principle' is often erroneously invoked to place limits on the behavior of some Christians whose conduct offends other Christians with stricter behavioral standards."[18] If we appeal to this passage, we are essentially identifying as the weaker member who needs extra grace from others.

We are free—to love and serve, not to cause others to stumble. As we consider stumbling blocks in gray areas, we must be careful how we implement Paul's instructions to the church at Corinth. The mature should not *always* yield to the immature or else the church would operate according to the weakest member.

Love asks for God's guidance to know when to set liberties aside and when to help a weaker or more sensitive sister or brother grow. Sometimes the most loving thing we can do is to kindly challenge weaker believers to embrace their Christian liberty. Other times we must set freedoms aside to love another well.

Paul said our failure to consider others might destroy weaker brothers and sisters. Jesus said it might destroy *us*.

Read the passage below, and circle the word *stumbling* every time you find it:

> [6] *"If any of you put a stumbling block before one of these little ones who believe in me, it would be better for you if a great millstone were fastened around your neck and you were drowned in the depth of the sea.* [7] *Woe to the world because of stumbling blocks! Occasions for stumbling are bound to come, but woe to the one by whom the stumbling block comes!"*
>
> *(Matthew 18:6-7 NRSV)*

What did Jesus say would be better than causing His little ones to stumble? (v. 6)

These words in Matthew 18 come right before the parable of the Good Shepherd, who leaves the ninety-nine to go after one stray sheep. As we follow Christ in valuing each person and treasuring the sanctity of his or her faith, Christ wants us to operate according to love. He died to give us liberty but cautions us to use our freedoms with care.

Gray issues can help us work through differences and give us an opportunity to sacrificially love our brothers and sisters in Christ. However, in the absence of love, the gray areas can destroy those weak in faith and pit us against each other.

> Sometimes the most loving thing we can do is to kindly challenge weaker believers to embrace their Christian liberty. Other times we must set freedoms aside to love another well.

> **Just because it seems "everybody's doing it" doesn't mean God is honored by it. . . . God longs for us to be set apart.**

I was talking to a young mom at church who recently brought her second baby home from the hospital. Her two-year-old daughter loved the baby at first, but after a few weeks she took a swing at the newborn. Even if it was jealousy that caused the toddler to lash out, the mom expressed her conflicted emotions as her beloved one whacked her new child. I wonder if this is how God feels when we hurt each other over things such as whether to celebrate Halloween, what age to allow our kids to date, or which shows we watch on television. Our squabbles destroy our unity—and could even cause others to stumble in faith. Jesus said a millstone around our neck is better than that! He's serious about our decisions and how they affect others.

This week we've learned that just because it seems "everybody's doing it" doesn't mean God is honored by it. Whether it's lawsuits, sexual sin, or exercising our personal freedoms without considering those weaker in faith, God longs for us to be set apart.

Talk with God

Spend some time in God's presence, praising Him for caring so deeply about each person that He is willing to leave the ninety-nine to go after the one. We all have been that one who needed to be pursued. Thank Him for places in your life where you see growth and transformation as you have matured in Christian liberties. Now ask Him to reveal any areas where your freedoms might be hurting other believers with weaker faith.

WEEKLY WRAP-UP

Note: This wrap-up exercise should take you approximately 6-7 minutes for reading the chapters and a few additional minutes for recording reflections.

Take a few minutes to read 1 Corinthians 6–8 again—either out loud if possible or silently if you are in a public setting.

What new insights or applications did the Holy Spirit lift off the page as you read?

Here are some of the highlights from our study this week:

- When believers sue one another, nobody wins. Sometimes God calls us to take a loss, and other times He asks us to stand up for injustice.

- In the midst of a culture obsessed with sex, the Lord calls us to run from sexual sin and honor Him with our bodies.
- God paid a high price for us, so we should see ourselves as valuable. He longs for us to be free in Christ rather than enslaved to sin.
- Some passages are prescriptive or true for all believers, and other verses include permissive instructions that might differ from person to person.
- Knowledge makes us feel important, but love strengthens the church. We shouldn't focus more on being right than showing love.
- We must be careful that our freedom in Christ doesn't cause a weaker Christian to stumble.

How do these themes both encourage and challenge you to live differently than the culture around you? What worldly thinking do you need to keep from creeping into your spiritual life and practice?

This week we've seen Paul help the Corinthians navigate gray issues, urging them not to fit in with the culture but to honor God and love others in their decisions. God's message hasn't changed when it comes to living counterculturally. We must be intentional and prepared so that we do not get sucked in by the strong pull of our culture. Instead we must learn to ask, "What will honor God and others?" as we seek the Spirit's help to live love. Even when God calls us to make different decisions, we can encourage and love one another in our pursuit of a close relationship with Jesus.

Digging Deeper

Paul's letter gives us a glimpse into the Corinthian church. Much has changed in the landscape of church life. What defines a church today? Can a Bible study or campus group be considered a church? Check out the online Digging Deeper article for Week 3, "Defining Church," to see what Scripture tells us about the church (see AbingdonPress.com /FirstCorinthians).

EVERYBODY'S DOING IT

"If any of you wants to be my follower, you must give up your own way, take up your cross daily, and follow me."

(Luke 9:23)

God calls us to _____ Him even when the winds of _____ are blowing in a totally different direction.

- Only Jesus satisfies our cravings—not the things of this world. (1 John 2:15-17)

- Paul urged the Corinthians not to fall back into old ways. (1 Corinthians 6:9-12)

We are to honor God with our _____.

- The Lord cares about our bodies. (1 Corinthians 6:13)

- The body, mind, and spirit are connected.

- Run from sexual sin; realize you are valuable; honor God with your body.

(1 Corinthians 6:18-20)

We are to _____ God's _____ for our particular situation.

3 Questions to ask when making decisions related to God's permissive will:

1. Will this absorb my _____ toward God or away from God?

(1 Corinthians 7:30-31)

- Will it draw me closer to Christ?

- Will it help me love God and others better?

- Is it something I want others to imitate?

2. Will this give me more _____?

(1 Corinthians 7:35)

3. Is this decision going to cause other people to _____?

(Romans 14:10, 12-13)

Now regarding your question about food that has been offered to idols. Yes, we know that "we all have knowledge" about this issue. But while knowledge makes us feel important, it is _____ that _____ the church. Anyone who claims to know all the answers doesn't really know very much. But the person who loves God is the one whom God recognizes.

(1 Corinthians 8:1-3)

Week 4

BEYOND OURSELVES

1 Corinthians 9–11

Memory Verses

22 When I am with those who are weak, I share their weakness, for I want to bring the weak to Christ. Yes, I try to find common ground with everyone, doing everything I can to save some. 23 I do everything to spread the Good News and share in its blessings.

(1 Corinthians 9:22-23)

DAY 1: SO WORTH IT

For many years I wasn't sure if I would be able to have children. When Sean and I were dating and it became clear that the relationship was getting serious, I had to initiate the "you might not have kids if you marry me" talk. Through tears I told him of my health struggles. He responded that he loved *me*, not my ability to produce offspring. Whatever we faced in the future we would face together as team Spoelstra.

Early in our marriage, we found that previous doctors weren't quite right in their assessment that medical intervention would be needed for us to get pregnant. We were ecstatic to find out that we would have a child much sooner than we had planned. Our first year of marriage had been blissful compared to the stories we heard of the difficulties others had in their first year. However, the easiness of marriage ended promptly when our amazing son entered the scene. Things we had counted as rights now had to be laid aside to take care of this new little person.

I had grown accustomed to things such as a good night's sleep, having a shower whenever I felt like it, sleeping in on Saturdays, and eating spicy food. All of a sudden these rights seemed like luxuries. The losses caused quite a bit of contention in our marriage as Sean and I adjusted to laying aside our rights for the benefit of our child and each other. No doubt you can relate—if not in parenting then in some other area of your life.

As we delve into 1 Corinthians 9–11 this week, we'll find God calling us to get beyond ourselves so that the gospel message can reach as many people as possible. Today as we study chapter 9, we will find three relevant principles for living this out.

1. Getting beyond ourselves requires giving up our rights.

Living love when we disagree sometimes means surrendering what we believe are rights or entitlements for the benefit of others. We might wonder, *How far should I go to accommodate the conscience of another person?* Paul answered this question by using his own life as an example. He began 1 Corinthians 9 with what reads like a resumé to convince the believers in the Corinthian church of his authority. He wanted them to see that surrendering his apostolic rights didn't diminish his apostolic authority.

Extra Insight

"Greeks despised manual labor. They had slaves to do manual labor so that the citizens could enjoy sports, philosophy, and leisure."[1]

Extra Insight

"The word *apostle* means 'one sent under commission' and refers primarily to the twelve apostles and Paul."[2]

Turn to 1 Corinthians 9 and put a placeholder there. Read verses 1 and 2, and check all the things Paul mentioned in regard to his authority:

__ Was free as anyone else

__ Had walked on water

__ Was an apostle

__ Had taken lots of missionary journeys

__ Had seen the Lord Jesus Christ with his own eyes

__ Was well liked by everyone

__ Was responsible for the Corinthians coming to know Christ

__ Was an eloquent teacher

After reminding the Corinthians that he retained apostolic status, Paul listed some of the rights that came with this office.

Read verses 3-6 and put a check next to the rights Paul mentioned in these verses:

__ To live in the homes of believers

__ To receive gifts during apostle's appreciation month

__ To have food and drink

__ To have a medical insurance plan

__ To take a believing wife along

__ To have four weeks of paid vacation

__ To work for a living

We also feel entitled to certain privileges associated with our jobs, positions, or roles. What are some things you expect as basic rights—either from an employer, the government, or a spouse or other family member?

As employees, many of us expect access to healthcare, prescriptions, bonuses, stock options, or overtime pay. As citizens, we might view electricity, clean water, and smoothly paved roads as rights. As members of families, we often consider things such as love, respect, encouragement, safety or security, and assistance or support as our rights.

Paul's life and writings affirm that it is normal to expect certain privileges associated with our position. In Acts 22:25, we discover that he claimed his rights as a Roman citizen when he was about to be whipped for preaching the gospel, demanding a trial before being punished based on his citizenship. And here in 1 Corinthians 9, he declared himself an apostle and explained the rights that usually accompanied apostleship. He also gave some examples of the benefits that came with certain jobs.

Read 1 Corinthians 9:7-14. Then draw a line to match each worker with a privilege associated with that position.

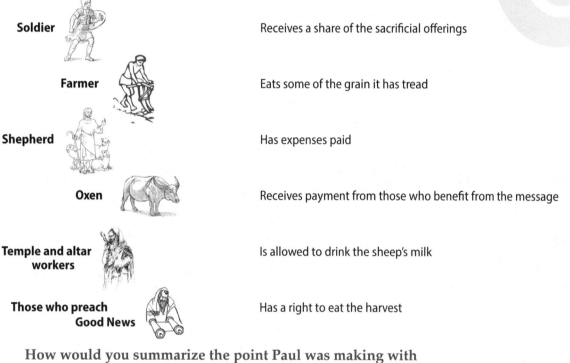

Soldier — Receives a share of the sacrificial offerings

Farmer — Eats some of the grain it has tread

Shepherd — Has expenses paid

Oxen — Receives payment from those who benefit from the message

Temple and altar workers — Is allowed to drink the sheep's milk

Those who preach Good News — Has a right to eat the harvest

How would you summarize the point Paul was making with these illustrations?

Paul made it clear that one should reap what one sows. As an apostle, he had a right to be paid. However, he laid aside that right of payment.

Read 1 Corinthians 9:15-23 and answer the following questions:

Why did Paul say he preached the gospel? (v. 16)

What did Paul claim was his pay? (v. 18)

Why did Paul say he had become a slave? (v. 19)

Even though he was free, Paul gave up all of his rights and became a slave in order to help people come to know Christ.

What things have you given up, or what personal inconveniences have you chosen, in order to share God's message with others—through words and/or service?

> **Surrendering our rights pales in comparison to what is gained when people encounter God's mercy and grace.**

When we sacrifice "me time" or add to an already packed schedule in order to prepare a Sunday school lesson, tutor an underprivileged child, or give a student a ride to youth group, we are making small sacrifices that God honors. Other times we may surrender big things in order to share the good news. Missionaries leave their families and homes. People refuse to compromise their beliefs, risking strained or broken relationships with friends or family members. Believers around the globe risk their safety by sharing the good news in hostile environments.

When our son, Zach, was born, we gave up many things we previously counted as rights very willingly for his sake. While our attitudes weren't always perfect, our great love for that little guy made it all worthwhile. Similarly, when it comes to sharing the gospel, God often calls us to give up our comfort or what we consider to be rights. But when we have an eternal perspective, we find that surrendering our rights pales in comparison to what is gained when people encounter God's mercy and grace. Though it's not always easy, Christ calls us to be willing to give up earthly entitlements so that others can hear the gospel message.

Take a moment to say a prayer, asking the Lord if He wants you to give up anything you have held on to as a "right." Now record any needed action steps or attitude adjustments that come to mind:

You may or may not have changes to make related to giving up your rights today, but it's a good practice to continually ask the Lord to reveal areas where you may be valuing your personal comfort over the development of your character. Paul learned that although sometimes we must assert our rights, other times we must give them up for the sake of the gospel.

2. Getting beyond ourselves requires finding common ground.

We find a second principle for getting beyond ourselves in chapter 9.

What did Paul claim that he tried to do according to 1 Corinthians 9:22-23?

Paul said he deferred to Jewish law when he was with Jews and lived apart from the law when he was with Gentiles so that he might find common ground with each group. Paul wasn't advocating being two-faced. Though he lived apart from the many Jewish laws when he was with the Gentiles, he did not break the law of Christ. He could obey Christ without following the letter of the Jewish law.

This principle resonates greatly in my life, as I hope it will in yours! As we seek to live love when we disagree, we can look for common ground in the midst of our differing viewpoints. Common ground is not middle ground where we compromise our beliefs; rather, it is ground where we affirm our shared beliefs.

In his book *The Politically Incorrect Jesus,* Joe Battaglia describes a discussion he had with someone who held an opposing viewpoint on a political issue. He writes,

> Middle ground suggests that we compromise on something we have no right in doing—violating our conscience and our understanding of God's Word. That's not finding middle ground; that's a sellout. Or intellectual dishonesty, at best....The higher ground is trying to find common ground so that even if we may not agree on a particular issue, we can still strive to find what we can agree on that satisfies both of our positions.[3]

When it comes to helping people come to know God, we can enter their world and look for common ground without compromising our views. As Paul said, he did everything he could to save some.

What are some practical ways you can look for common ground with someone you know who does not follow Christ?

> Common ground is not middle ground where we compromise our beliefs; rather, it is ground where we affirm our shared beliefs.

We aren't talking about faking interest in others just so we can tally up witnessing experiences. Paul didn't bait and switch.

Once when my kids were small, I had a rare opportunity to go to the grocery store alone. I wandered the aisles—excited that no one was bickering or sneaking Twinkies into the cart. A woman approached me and told me how great I looked. As a mom of four who lived in sweats and ponytails, I blushed and accepted the compliment. She continued to make small talk, asking me questions and seeming to be truly interested in my life. Then she mentioned that she needed models for her business, and she asked if I would come to a meeting where she would demonstrate a skin care line. I realized then that I'd been suckered. Her compliments had an end game of me buying her products. I felt conned and even angry.

I have talked with atheist friends who have felt these same feelings toward well-meaning Christians who have made them feel like projects—friends who are chosen so that they can be changed in some way. People are not projects!

My husband and I have invited several of our atheist neighbors to church parties or functions. One time a couple from across the street came to our small group Christmas party. They met many of our friends and seemed to make connections and enjoy themselves. When we invited them to the group's next Bible study series, they asked if we could still be friends without "church stuff." They weren't interested in Jesus but wondered if we could continue our relationship. They were asking if they were just projects or if we were interested in genuine friendship with no strings attached. We assured them we cared about them whether they joined our group or not, and we continued to invite them to dinner and parties to demonstrate our feelings.

When it comes to sharing our faith, Paul demonstrated finding common ground by becoming others-centered. In our conversations, we should seek to connect with others based on their background and interests rather than our interests or experiences. William Barclay once said, "One of our greatest necessities is to learn the art of getting along with people; and so often the trouble is that we do not even try."[4] Trying to get along begins with shifting our focus from self to others.

In Romans 12:9 we read, "Don't just pretend to love others. Really love them. Hate what is wrong. Hold tightly to what is good." As Christ-followers, we invest in relationships and invite others to know and love God because we care about them. I want everyone I love to know Christ. I can't imagine life without Him—for this life or the next. I believe that sin separates us from God and Christ reconciles us to God. However, I must not pretend to be interested in people's lives so that I can try to sell them on Jesus. I must truly love them.

God calls us to treasure one another. I pray that will be something you will always remember from our study of Paul's letter to the church in Corinth. Even the person you seem to have nothing in common with has

> **Trying to get along begins with shifting our focus from self to others.**

a desire to be loved and validated. Everyone wants to feel that he or she matters.

Jesus *offers* Himself to everyone; He doesn't *force* Himself on anyone. As Christ-followers, we shouldn't force Christ on anyone either. Rather, as we genuinely treasure and love people, we can find common ground that allows us to share the good news with them.

Think of two people you know who do not follow Christ, and spend a few minutes praying for them right now. Write their names or initials in the margin. What is one way you can reach out to them this week to show your sincere love for them?

Most people have a pretty good gauge for sensing when we really care or just want to convince them of our way of thinking. As we seek to find common ground, let's not pretend to love people but really love them! We can build a bridge of love from our hearts to theirs—and then let Jesus walk across.

3. Getting beyond ourselves requires staying spiritually fit.

Paul ends chapter 9 describing the intensity with which we are called to spread the Good News.

Read 1 Corinthians 9:24-27 and summarize below what Paul said:

Corinth hosted the Isthmian Games, which were second only to the Olympics. So Paul related to the Corinthian church by using an example that hit close to home—a foot race, which was the main event of the games. Athletes in Corinth trained and disciplined themselves to win. The prize for winning an event wasn't a gold, silver, or bronze medal that would last. It was a crown made of laurel leaves that faded away with time. Paul reminded the Corinthians again to pursue things that would last forever.

If athletes in Corinth worked so hard to gain a temporary prize, how much more disciplined should we be to store up treasure in heaven that will last forever?

What will last forever, remaining throughout eternity? What are some things that are only temporary?

Eternal   **Temporary**

Extra Insight

"Held every three years in honor of Poseidon, the Greek god of the sea, the Isthmian Games were the centerpiece of Corinthian civic pride."[5]

Paul acknowledged that taking care of the body has value, saying that physical discipline and training yield benefits. Yet compared to the spiritual, the physical is fleeting.

Like the Corinthians, we live in a culture obsessed with outward appearances. Though taking care of our bodies is a worthwhile pursuit, we cannot lose sight of the fact that our bodies will fade away like the laurel leaves in the crowns won at the Isthmian Games. Because our bodies are temporary, we should give our time and attention to spiritual training, realizing those investments are eternal.

What spiritual disciplines do you regularly practice to stay strong spiritually? How have these spiritual disciplines impacted your spiritual growth in the last year?

Keeping our eyes focused on the goal of growing strong spiritually in order to be equipped to share the gospel with others gives us staying power when we grow weary in our spiritual training. As believers, we must remind one another that praying, reading and studying the Bible, memorizing Scripture, taking time for rest, meeting together with our church family, sharing our testimonies, and finding common ground with those who don't know Christ are things that will echo into eternity. Focusing on spiritual growth helps us remember that we aren't just spinning our wheels in our Christian walk. Like an athlete training for the Olympics, we are to set our sights on eternity and run the race to win the prize of seeing more people come to know and follow Jesus.

Throughout chapter 9 we find Paul giving instructions that will help the Corinthian believers spread the gospel.

Giving up our rights, finding common ground, and staying spiritually fit will equip us to spread the gospel message in our spheres of influence. Implementing these principles yields rewards that are greater than we can imagine in this life and that echo into eternity.

Talk with God

Take a few moments to ask yourself where God might be asking you to make any changes in your attitudes, words, or actions regarding the three principles in today's lesson, and then listen for His voice. Make notes in the margin if you like.

DAY 2: CAUTION SIGNS

I love my kids so much sometimes that it literally hurts my heart. I look back at pictures of them when they were little and remember how they said things like "skabetti" for spaghetti and promised they would live in my house forever. My "littles" have grown past the days of mispronounced words and rash vows. They now face challenges in middle school, high school, and college—where potential dangers abound. I remind them of godly young men and women who lived victoriously for God and changed the world. Not only do I want them to hear these inspiring stories, but I also want them to know the heartbreaking accounts of those who lived for themselves and reaped the consequences. Experience is a great teacher, but I'd rather they not have to get in the sewer in order to know it stinks!

After talking about giving up rights, finding common ground, and staying spiritually fit, Paul moved on to warn the church at Corinth about some pitfalls that would inhibit the church from standing together for the gospel.

Paul was a learned Jewish scholar. According to Acts 22:3, he studied under a Pharisee named Gamaliel, who was an expert in Jewish law. From Paul's study of the Scriptures, he knew that idolatry, immorality, and a complaining spirit could ruin a group of believers and derail them from accomplishing the purpose God had given them. So he wanted the Corinthians to learn from past mistakes in the faith community.

Turn to 1 Corinthians 10 and put a placeholder there. Then read verses 1-5. What story from biblical history did Paul reference?

In the Books of Exodus and Numbers, we find the account of Israel's wilderness wanderings. Their journey out of Egyptian slavery wasn't uncomplicated or short. Here are some highlights from the story:

- After God miraculously brought ten plagues on Egypt and Pharaoh let the Hebrew slaves go, Moses led them through the Red Sea to freedom. (Exodus 7–14)
- God instructed Moses to send twelve spies to survey the Promised Land, and ten of them gave a bad report, saying they would lose if they fought. Only Caleb and Joshua suggested they believe God and take the land. (Numbers 13)
- Because of their lack of trust and obedience, God sent them to wander in the wilderness for forty years. (Numbers 14)
- During those years of wilderness wanderings, God provided food (manna and quail) and water for His people. (Exodus 15–17)
- The people complained about the food (Exodus 16), asked Aaron to make them a golden calf to worship (Exodus 32), and engaged in sexual sin (Numbers 25).
- The Lord loved, disciplined, and provided for the people until the older generation died off and the next generation was ready to go in and take the land under Joshua's leadership. (Joshua 1)

Extra Insight

The first four verses of 1 Corinthians 10 are a single sentence in the Greek.[6]

Chapter 10 opens with Paul saying, "I don't want you to forget, dear brothers and sisters, about our ancestors in the wilderness long ago" (v. 1). The Israelites had witnessed God deliver them through the Red Sea, but as Warren Wiersbe points out, "good beginnings do not guarantee good endings."[7]

Why do you think Paul wanted the Corinthian believers to remember this particular account? (Answers will vary. Simply share your own thoughts.)

Personally, I wonder if Paul referenced the Israelites' wilderness wanderings because their story reveals that they struggled with some of the same sins that were issues for the Corinthian believers—including these three:

1. Idolatry. The Israelites in the wilderness set up an idol, a golden calf, to worship, while the Corinthian Christians struggled with what to do about meat sacrificed to idols.

2. Immorality. God reprimanded the Israelites for immorality when they brazenly engaged in sexual relations with people they camped near in the wilderness. Paul also addressed the sexual sin of the Corinthian believers, including the man who was living with his stepmother in an incestuous relationship.

3. A complaining spirit. The Israelites in the wilderness complained about food, living conditions, and their leaders. The Corinthians played favorites with leaders and brought lawsuits against each other.

Paul referred to the Israelites' struggles in these areas as he warned the Corinthians to learn from their example. He didn't want only behavior modification for the Corinthians; he wanted to get to the heart of the issue. So he used the example of the Israelites in the wilderness to help the church dig beneath the surface, exposing the dangers of idolatry, immorality, and a complaining spirit. While our circumstances may not be similar to those of the wandering Israelites or the church at Corinth, all of us can learn to heed God's caution signs to keep from embracing counterfeits, impurity, and a lack of contentment.

What cautions do you need to heed in your current circumstances related to each of these dangers?

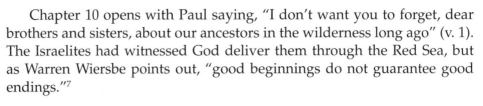

CAUTION
Immorality

CAUTION
Complaining Spirit

Good beginnings in the Corinthian church did not guarantee good outcomes. Recognizing that the church in Corinth faced many of the same issues that confronted the Israelites during their wilderness wanderings, Paul wanted them to be aware of the potential pitfalls and consequences.

Read 1 Corinthians 10:6-13. What reason did Paul give for this history lesson? (vv. 6, 11)

Like a father who was warning his children, Paul reminded the church of past consequences for those who had dabbled with disobedience.

God forgives our sin, but consequences can remain for decades in the wake of bad decisions. Proverbs 1:31 says this of those who hate knowledge and reject wisdom's advice: "Therefore, they must eat the bitter fruit of living their own way, choking on their own schemes."

Paul didn't want to watch his beloved children in the Lord eating the bitter fruit of living their own way—just as we hope to spare our children from making dangerous decisions. As we read the Corinthians' mail, we hear God's message to us about living carefully. We, too, need "caution signs" regarding these three sin tendencies in our lives. Let's take a look at each of these sin tendencies and consider what we can learn so that we do not repeat the mistakes of those who have gone before us.

1. Idolatry

In 1 Corinthians 10:6-7, Paul referenced the Israelites' struggle with idolatry in the wilderness as he warned the Corinthians about craving evil things and worshiping idols. While the Corinthians lived in a city where idol worship entailed sacrificial butcher shops and temple prostitution, our own brand of idolatry looks quite different. We don't have to debate whether we should eat meat offered to false gods or bow down to statues, but the temptation to allow earthly things to take God's place in our hearts is real.

Read Colossians 3:5 in the margin. How does this verse describe idolatry?

When we elevate the *created* above the *Creator*, we engage in idolatry. Idols can even be people or resources given by God that we hold too tightly. Tim Keller defines idolatry as "anything more important to you than God, anything that absorbs your heart and imagination more than God, anything you seek to give you what only God can give."[8]

What things are competing for God's place in your heart?

> **When we elevate the *created* above the *Creator*, we engage in idolatry.**

God reminds us of the dangers of idolatry not only for ourselves but also for the entire community of believers. Some of my personal idols include productivity, comfort, and approval. When I'm looking for validation in what I do, how I feel, or how others see me, I am very "me" focused. Idolatry keeps me stuck in my own head, unable to engage in God's mission of sharing His love with the world.

How would you describe the difference between a day when your personal idols keep you focused inward and a day when your resolve to put God first gives you an outward focus? (Think about what is different in your thought life, attitude, words, and actions.)

God's warnings about idolatry are not meant to shame us but to remind us to keep Him first so that we can live abundant lives rather than experience the soul sickness that comes with counterfeits.

2. Immorality

In addition to addressing sexual immorality in chapter 6, where he reminded the Corinthians to honor God with their bodies (v. 20), Paul warned them again in chapter 10 to avoid sexual sin by referring to the example of the Israelites in the wilderness (v. 8). The story of the Israelites' sin, found in Numbers 25, reminds us that God loves us desperately and knows that sexual immorality isn't good for us.

Read Ephesians 5:3 in the margin. According to this verse, why are we to avoid sexual sin?

Sexual sin has destroyed the lives of so many men and women of God. The enemy uses the weakness of our flesh to tempt us, especially when we are seeking to serve God. Knowing this, we should be on guard against sexual sin. We may think we are above these temptations, but God warns us to stay humble and dependent on Him so that we don't sin sexually. My prayer is that God will help us eliminate even a hint of sexual sin in our lives as we yield to Him. God gives us grace when we fall and restores us as we repent; however, we should constantly pursue sexual purity so that we can avoid the pitfalls of this destructive sin and be effective witnesses for the gospel.

It can be challenging to keep our thought lives, media choices, and reading material from having even a hint of immorality. Though God doesn't want us to get tripped up in legalistic rules in our pursuit of purity, He does want us to recognize the contagious nature of sin in our lives and be on guard against it. Though we won't find purity in our own strength, through the power of Christ and the Holy Spirit we can learn from the past and find greater freedom in the future.

Pause and say a short prayer, asking God to give you purity of heart and mind so that your witness for Christ won't contain even a hint of immorality. If you like, write it in the margin.

3. A Complaining Spirit

Another warning Paul gave the Corinthians as he mentioned the Israelites' time in the wilderness hits close to home for us. They grumbled and complained. God gave the Israelites food from heaven each morning in the form of manna, but the Israelites were not content and longed for the vegetables they had had in Egypt. They looked back on slavery with rose-colored glasses, and they grumbled against Moses.

Read Numbers 14:1-5 and list their complaints:

Later in Numbers 14 we see that the Israelites actually discussed stoning Moses and Aaron. Paul related their grumblings to the church in Corinth, who were squabbling over leadership and possessions. They did not get along, sued each other, and were dissatisfied with what they had.

Though God doesn't want us to get tripped up in legalistic rules in our pursuit of purity, He does want us to recognize the contagious nature of sin in our lives and be on guard against it.

Extra Insight

The word *manna* in Hebrew means "What is it?"[9] It tasted like wafers made with honey and looked like coriander seed (Exodus 16:31).

"We often judge the outside of someone else's family against the inside of ours."
—Mary Beth

As you consider your own spiritual life, do you ever find yourself battling a lack of contentment regarding what God has provided for you? We can be tempted to look around and think everyone else has better houses, food, jobs, churches, bodies, and families.

Social media shows us pictures of everyone with their best foot forward. While we celebrate the successes of friends and family, we must guard against comparing and complaining. My friend Mary Beth shared with me a statement that I can relate to as someone who is prone to compare. She said, "We often judge the outside of someone else's family against the inside of ours." This leads to skewed measurement. When the grass seems greener somewhere else, it's time to water our own spiritual yards.

Paul said this about contentment in a letter to his protégé, Timothy: "Yet true godliness with contentment is itself great wealth" (1 Timothy 6:6). In other words, great wealth is found in godliness coupled with contentment.

How would you define the word *contentment*?

As I have discussed the subject of contentment with others, I've found that some people mistakenly associate the word with laziness or being idle. Complacency and contentment, however, are two different things. Being content doesn't mean sitting back and doing nothing in the midst of the struggles of life. It means accepting God's provision in our lives rather than grumbling about what we think we lack.

Think of an area in your life where you are struggling with contentment. Ask God to help you learn from the mistakes of the Israelites and the Corinthian believers. Write a short prayer below, asking God for eyes to see the good He is working in your life:

If we look for the good, we will surely find it; and if we look for the bad, we will surely find it. God calls us to find satisfaction in Him instead of grumbling and complaining.

The Scriptures give us warnings and examples to help us avoid repeating the mistakes of our ancestors. We must guard against idolatry, immorality, and a complaining spirit so that we can get beyond ourselves and spend our energies sharing the gospel message and the love of Christ with a world in need.

Which of these three sin tendencies resonates most strongly with you? Circle the word below, and write one action step that you can take this week to get beyond yourself in this area.

Idolatry   Immorality   A Complaining Spirit

In 1 Corinthians 10:12, we read, "If you think you are standing strong, be careful not to fall." Paul knew that "pride goes before destruction [and haughtiness before a fall]" (Proverbs 16:18). Living love requires humble dependence on Christ and a teachable spirit.

As we wrap up today's lesson, let's be encouraged by the reminder that through Christ we can achieve victory over these sins that threaten our unity in the body.

Write 1 Corinthians 10:13 below:

What good news! God will provide "a way out"! I love this insight from William Barclay related to this verse: "The word that Paul uses is vivid (*ekbasis*). It means *a way out of a mountain pass*. The idea is of an army apparently surrounded and then suddenly seeing an escape route to safety."[10] God promises that in those situations when we feel we are about to give in to temptation, He will always provide an escape route.

I've often heard people misquote this verse by saying, "God will never give you more than you can handle." That is *not* what this verse says. I don't know about you, but God constantly gives me more than I can handle: knowing how to parent in difficult situations; counseling women in times of heartbreak; keeping my marriage a priority amidst family and ministry responsibilities; maintaining a consistent prayer life; keeping my house clean, the laundry done, and food on the table.

What is your list of things you can't handle without God's help?

1.

2.

3.

I often feel stretched by much more than I can handle emotionally, physically, spiritually, and mentally. But when I recognize that my life is more than I can handle, that's when God shows up in the biggest ways!

The sin struggles of the Israelites in the wilderness that Paul referred to in 1 Corinthians 10 remind us of our need to stay dependent on the Lord. We can't handle it all, but He can. God often gives us more than we can manage, but He never tempts us to sin. In fact, He shows us an escape route so that we do not have to fall into "the sin that so easily entangles" us (Hebrews 12:1 NIV).

Whether we are struggling with idolatry, immorality, a complaining spirit, or any other sin that crouches at our door, God can give us power over it. First Corinthians 10:13 reminds us that we are not alone in our temptations. Others experience them too. And God will faithfully provide a way out for us. We do not have to stay in the defeating cycle of sin!

Like my mother's heart hurts for my kids, our heavenly Father's heart bursts with love for us. I'm thankful that He not only warns us of the dangers of sin but offers us a way to be victorious over it!

Talk with God

Invite God to point out any areas where you need a warning. Ask Him to use His Word, His people, and the quiet voice of His Spirit to speak to you today and in the days ahead. Thank Him that He loves you enough to warn you about the dangers of idolatry, immorality, and a complaining spirit.

DAY 3: OFFENDED

Sean and I bought our first home when our son, Zach, was two years old. We were excited to plant flowers, paint walls, and get to know our neighbors. The first invitation of any sort that I received was to trick or treat with the mom and daughter who lived next door. I told Sean about the invitation, and together we discussed our options and prayed.

We could darken our house and explain to our neighbor that as Christians we didn't want to participate in this holiday. Instead we decided to dress our son up in a cute costume. Sean passed out candy at our home, and I walked with my new friend, meeting the people who lived in the homes in our neighborhood. For the next decade, my neighbor and I kept this tradition, ending up at one of our houses for hot cocoa while our children sorted their candy. After she moved over an hour away, she continued to drive back with her kids to walk our old beat together on trick-or-treat night.

At times during those years, families at church asked us whether we allowed our children to participate in Halloween or beggar's night. We offended some when we told them we did. My husband would try to make it lighthearted by exclaiming with a laugh, "If they are going to pass out free candy in our neighborhood, I'm going to send my kids out to get it for me!"

God has led many wonderful believers we know to abstain from participating in Halloween activities. Some friends have fall celebrations at their church in lieu of trick or treating so that their children won't be exposed to scary costumes or decorations. We have close family members who have strong feelings against any kind of participation. How we handle Halloween illustrates a wisdom issue where Christians often disagree.

What are some of the wisdom issues—preferences or gray areas—on which Christians often have different views?

I posted this question online, and here are some of the responses I received:

- Drinking alcohol in moderation
- Watching R-rated movies
- Singing hymns vs. contemporary praise and worship songs
- Determining the appropriate age to let kids date
- Reading non-Christian books
- Working outside the home as a mom
- Making education choices (public school, Christian school, homeschool)
- Getting vaccines
- Choosing traditional or alternative medical practices
- Selecting a Bible translation
- Honoring the Sabbath
- Making pregnancy and baby decisions (whether to have an epidural, breastfeed, use a pacifier, and so on)
- Allowing kids to participate in travel sports
- Choosing/listening to secular music
- Teaching kids about Santa or the Easter bunny
- Making choices regarding jewelry and make-up

And this isn't all of the responses! One woman even said she observed Christian women arguing on Facebook about whether or not to assist your child on the monkey bars. Clearly we disagree about a lot of things! Having differences of opinion is nothing new. The Corinthian Christians had their own divisive issues. Let's look at some guiding principles to help us navigate gray areas.

Yesterday we saw that Paul warned the Corinthians of the dangers of idolatry, immorality, and a complaining spirit. He encouraged them with the truth that God always provides a way out when we are tempted. Today we will see how he helped them apply these truths in a particular situation they faced: whether to eat meat that had been sacrificed to idols.

Paul told the Corinthian believers that they were reasonable people (1 Corinthians 10:15). He had expressed earlier in his letter that they had been given the mind of Christ (1 Corinthians 2:16), and now he wanted them to weigh the facts and decide for themselves. So he made some arguments both for and against the practice.

Read 1 Corinthians 10:14-23 and label each of the following arguments either a PRO or CON for eating meat that had been sacrificed to idols:

1. _____ **Food offered to idols has no significance, because the idols that the food is offered to aren't real gods.**

2. _____ **The food is sacrificed to demons.**

3. _____ **Eating the meat could rouse God's jealousy.**

4. _____ **I am allowed to do anything.**

5. _____ **Not everything is good for me.**

Numbers 1 and 4 are PROs, suggesting that no harm would come from eating meat sacrificed to idols. Numbers 2, 3, and 5 are CONs, giving reasons to avoid the practice.

Freedom in Christ makes all matters of conscience permissible, but we must take time to reason, pray, and search the Scriptures to discern whether a particular activity is beneficial.

Consider the decisions you have made in some of the gray areas included in the bulleted list. What helped you discern your personal position?

We must be careful about proof-texting when it comes to these issues. Proof-texting means deciding what you believe and then going back to find verses to support that position. The problem with proof-texting is that verses taken out of context can seem to contradict each other.

Consider the two statements of Paul in the margin. How do these verses seem to say contradictory things?

Paul isn't contradicting himself; he is just emphasizing that God's approval is more important than people's opinions. However, he prioritizes helping others find their way to God over what is best for him. Context

Obviously, I'm not trying to win the approval of people, but of God. If pleasing people were my goal, I would not be Christ's servant.
(Galatians 1:10)

I, too, try to please everyone in everything I do. I don't just do what is best for me; I do what is best for others so that many may be saved.
(1 Corinthians 10:33)

is important. Rather than start with our position and work backward, we should come to the text humbly and with an open mind and heart, asking God to show us His heart and will for us. God calls us to be teachable, able to flex our spiritual muscles in new directions as we grow in Him.

Paul showed that the issue of meat sacrificed to idols required different stances depending on the situation.

Read 1 Corinthians 10:24-30 and fill in the chart below:

Verse(s)	Situation	What to do	Because
25-26	Eat meat sold in marketplace	Don't raise questions of conscience	The earth is the Lord's and everything in it
27			(not listed)
28-29			

Paul wasn't a proponent of situational ethics, which is determining what is ethical according to context rather than principle. Rather, he wanted the Corinthians to get beyond themselves and consider others when making decisions. We too should consider others when making decisions about issues of personal preference or conscience. The following chart shows how I did that related to the observance of Halloween.

Situation	What to do	Because
Neighbor invites me to trick or treat with kids.	Decide to dress up kids and go.	Opportunity to build long-term relationships with neighbors.
Relative visits with children on Halloween and is against participating in the holiday.	Decide to attend a fall festival or participate in other fun activity away from neighborhood instead.	Don't want to offend my relative's conscience or cause awkward situation for the children.

Now it's your turn. Think of an issue that you might respond to differently depending on the situation. Fill in the following chart:

Situation	What to do	Because

In the last few verses of chapter 10, we find some overarching principles to guide us as we seek God's help in navigating the choppy waters of divisive issues.

Read 1 Corinthians 10:31-33 and write two statements to sum up Paul's advice:

1.

2.

As we make decisions about anything from our children's education to media choices, Paul says we should ask ourselves:

- What will glorify the Lord?
- How will this decision affect others?

These two questions remind me of a simple acronym I learned at church camp when I was young. The leader taught that the order of our life should be:

1. **J**esus
2. **O**thers
3. **Y**ou

If you put the first letter of each of those words together, what word does it spell?

Our culture tells us to put ourselves first, but Jesus shows us that real joy comes when we put God first, consider others in our decisions, and then evaluate what is best for us.

Take a moment now to identify another gray area (different from the one you identified previously) where you aren't sure what to do. Write the scenario below:

Now ask yourself the two questions we gleaned from 1 Corinthians 10:31-33 in regard to this gray area:

What will glorify the Lord in this situation?

> Our culture tells us to put ourselves first, but Jesus shows us that real joy comes when we put God first, consider others in our decisions, and then evaluate what is best for us.

How will this decision benefit or offend others?

Oftentimes we seem to be in a no-win situation. If we proceed, we might offend one group of believers; but if we refrain, we might offend those we are seeking to reach with the gospel. These two questions may lead us to different conclusions in different situations. We need the help of the Spirit to lead us individually. Then we can confidently hold to our decision even when others come against it. We will experience greater JOY when we seek to put Jesus first and consider the benefit of others.

When it comes to gray areas, we aren't alone in our struggle to honor God and consider how our decisions affect others. In matters of conscience we may be allowed to do anything, but not everything will be beneficial. Sometimes we have to make tough choices between liberty and influence. We are free, but not to hurt others with our liberty. Instead, we must seek to honor God and others and take a gracious posture toward those who disagree with our decisions.

Talk with God

Spend some time in God's presence, asking Him to give you further discernment regarding any area in your life where you aren't sure how to proceed. Ask Him: How can I bring you glory in my decision? How will others be encouraged in their faith by my decision? How can I imitate Jesus as I approach this issue or topic?

DAY 4: INTERDEPENDENT

After Paul told the Corinthians to seek God's glory and consider others' feelings and perspectives in gray areas, he transitioned into the subject of head coverings—discussing why women should wear them but men should not. Part of me would like to skip these verses because of the controversy and debate surrounding them. But our theme this week is getting beyond ourselves so that we can seek harmony in the church and together share the good news about Christ. So let's take a fresh look at Paul's words with curiosity and a teachable spirit. As we explore some cultural perspectives that might be foreign to us regarding head coverings, hair, and worship practices during the days of the early church in Corinth, we'll discover what these verses can teach us about unity in the body of Christ.

Read 1 Corinthians 11:1-16 and write below any questions or comments that these verses bring to mind:

Extra Insight

Sometimes division can arise because of semantics. We may be saying the same thing but defining our words differently. Other times we truly disagree and must lovingly accept one another as we maintain different views. Here are some guidelines to follow before responding:

1. Clarify words and seek to understand.
2. Ask more questions.
3. Get counsel from trusted advisors.
4. Pray and wait twenty-four hours.
5. Be kind and direct when explaining concerns.

These verses contain some statements that are confusing to us and raise a number of questions. When we read them without attempting to understand the cultural context, we set ourselves up for misinterpretation and misunderstanding.

As I was leading the pilot group for this study, I decided to invite the group—which included women of different ages and levels of spiritual maturity with varied denominational backgrounds—to dig into several commentaries with me.[11] I gave each woman two or three commentaries and asked her to read the notes pertaining to 1 Corinthians 11:1-16 and then answer two questions. (This may be something you and your group want to do as well.) When we gathered to share our findings, we had some rich and enlightening discussion.

Let's look at the two questions together and consider what applications we can find that resonate in our lives. While we may not find specific direction or guidance for our own personal situations, we will grow in our understanding of how cultural customs can impact spiritual decisions.

The first question we discussed has to do with cultural context.

1. What cultural understandings from this time period give us insight into Paul's instructions in these verses?

Though there is debate among scholars regarding cultural practices and understandings related to head coverings in Corinth at this time, here are some insights the women in our group discovered from the Bible commentaries we consulted:

- It was considered dishonoring or shameful for women not to cover their heads in prayer. Loose and flowing hair symbolized that the women themselves were loose from social constraints.
- Some scholars say that loose and flowing hair was a sign of an unmarried, adulterous, or pagan woman.
- The culture of the day had a very low view of women. While sometimes Paul seems sexist in his writings, he actually elevated women by encouraging them to learn and pointing out their value. When he said that men were not independent of women but needed them (v. 11), this would have been shocking and affirming to women.
- It was considered natural or proper for Jewish men to have short hair. Long hair or a covered head would have been considered disgraceful for a man. (Only men who took a Nazarite vow—a vow taken by individuals who voluntarily dedicated themselves to God—typically had longer hair.)

How do these cultural insights help you better understand this passage?

When we understand the culture of the original audience, we find that this passage isn't about the subordination of women but about keeping order and maintaining honor. For the Corinthian believers, obeying these instructions meant aligning with customary practice. Paul affirmed the women's value but reminded them that some gender distinctions and cultural practices needed to be upheld for the sake of order and harmony.

In verses 14 and 15 we read, "Isn't it obvious that it's disgraceful for a man to have long hair? And isn't long hair a woman's pride and joy? For it has been given to her as a covering." The words "isn't it obvious" reveal the culture wrapped in Paul's instructions. For us, this might be similar to a student forgetting to take off his baseball cap during the national anthem at a sporting event and someone reminding him of the custom by saying, "Isn't it obvious that you should take off your hat in respect?"

In verse 16, Paul himself referred to the instructions regarding head coverings as a custom or practice rather than a command. Let's compare the Greek word that Paul used here for *custom* to the Greek word he used elsewhere in his letter for *command*.

Greek Word	Definition	Where Used
Sunetheia[13]	Intimacy, custom, a being used to, accustomed	1 Corinthians 11:16
Epitage[14]	Mandate, commandment, injunction	1 Corinthians 7:6 and 7:25

Why do you think it is significant that Paul used *sunetheia* to refer to the instructions regarding head coverings rather than *epitage*?

Paul could have chosen *epitage* to command women to cover their heads, but instead he chose *sunetheia*, signifying that it was an accepted custom or practice. Throughout the centuries, cultural customs have changed. However, commandments of God transcend time and culture, and we guard these truths from cultural shifts. Truth does not change, but how we apply those truths in each generation does. So, as most commentators agree, our application of these verses today does not result in women wearing head coverings and men cutting their hair short.

At the time of Paul's writing, men who practiced Judaism and men who followed Christ (many of whom were Jews) did not cover their heads during prayer, while women in both faith communities did. Yet around

Extra Insight

The topic of gender roles has threatened to divide believers throughout church history. But in 1 Corinthians 11:1-16, Paul is not speaking about the roles or positions of women in the church but about the customs of women and men during prayer.

Extra Insight

"It is possible that Paul may someday be discovered as the great emancipator and protector of woman."[15]
—Charles Erdman

the fourth century, men who practiced Judaism began wearing a small round cap during prayer,[16] signifying a change in custom for those of the Jewish faith. Though Christian women continued to wear head coverings (and later hats) in worship into the twentieth century, this practice is no longer customary among most Christian women today. Again, the custom changed. So are we to toss this passage aside as no longer relevant?

As 2 Timothy 3:16 tells us, all Scripture is God-breathed and useful for teaching. This leads us to the second question our group explored.

2. What biblical principles do we find in these verses, and how can we apply them in our own lives?

While the diverse group of gals sat in my living room discussing 1 Corinthians 11:1-16 and the commentaries we had read, we looked for statements or thoughts that we could apply to any culture or era. Three principles rose to the top in our collective conversation.

1. Men and women have equality in worth and value, but God created us with feminine and masculine distinctions. Going all the way back to the creation account, we find that God made men and women unique. Genesis 1:27 tells us, "So God created human beings in his own image. In the image of God he created them; male and female he created them."

Recently my husband, Sean, had oral surgery to have a tooth extracted. Before the surgery he expressed concerns that he might hear crunching noises as they worked and shared that he was considering general anesthesia. As he expressed his honest fears, I tried to listen compassionately, but he sensed my inaudible chuckle and said, "What?" I admitted that it was weird for me to see my big, strong husband expressing his concerns over a dental procedure. We both laughed when I said, "Never have a baby." He promised to comply. While men and women may have varied approaches to dental work, we can all agree that only women know the joys and pains of pregnancy, labor, and the delivery of a baby.

Men and women are different. Though I believe in equal rights for men and women, our culture's fight for equality between the sexes can sometimes cross the line, attempting to eliminate all gender distinctions. Paul's instructions encouraged the church in Corinth to continue customary practices that honored gender distinctions between men and women. Galatians 3:28 tells us that "there is no longer Jew or Gentile, slave or free, male and female. For you are all one in Christ Jesus." Certainly we find equality at the foot of the cross, but we also retain our uniqueness.

2. Though Paul writes of subordination in divine and human relationships, God-honoring, willing submission never determines or lessens value. Submission has become a loaded word today, carrying the connotation of being a doormat or having lesser value. But we know that this is not the case because of what we find in the Godhead.

Read John 10:30 and John 14:28 in the margin. What do you learn from these verses about the relationship between Jesus and the Father?

"The Father and I are one." (John 10:30)

"Remember what I told you: I am going away, but I will come back to you again. If you really loved me, you would be happy that I am going to the Father, who is greater than I am." (John 14:28)

Jesus affirmed that He and the Father were one while acknowledging that God the Father was greater than He—not in worth or power, but in position. Similarly, when Paul wrote about the subordination in divine and human relationships (1 Corinthians 11:3), he was not diminishing women but merely pointing out that God's design in all relationships—whether they be in an organization, a church, or even a family—includes a structure of responsibility. Though we may see Paul's words as demeaning today, in the cultural context in which he was writing, he was actually lifting up the value of women by acknowledging that men were dependent on them (1 Corinthians 11:11-12). I wonder if the Corinthian women weren't fist bumping each other as they heard this public affirmation. The concept of the interdependence of men and women would have been radical in that time of history.

At any given time, each person is subordinate to someone—whether it be a parent, teacher, boss, police officer, or another individual. What's most important is the relationship of the two people, not their roles or responsibilities.

How is God calling you to embrace humility in a relationship of subordination or willing submission—whether at work or church, in a volunteer organization, or in a family situation?

3. We need to consider when it is appropriate to adapt to customary practices. Though clearly Paul thought it was right for women to cover their heads in worship and men to have shorter hair—and stacked up arguments why they should comply—he also invited the Christians in Corinth to think about this issue themselves when he said, "Judge for yourselves..." (1 Corinthians 11:13). It is possible that when he thought about Christian women with uncovered heads in worship, he was concerned not only about their honor and what was proper but also about their witness to the watching world. As I've mentioned, some scholars have suggested that women with uncovered heads might have been associated with immoral women. Although we do not know all of Paul's motives here, we do know from earlier comments in his letter that he wanted the Corinthians to consider others when making decisions.

We must judge for ourselves when it is appropriate to follow customary practices and when it is not. As we strive to be relevant, we will need the Lord's help to know where the boundary lines are, separating our freedom in Christ and sin.

Though we live in more of an "anything goes" culture today with fewer specifics regarding propriety, we can relate to the idea of being willing to consider others when making decisions about customs. When I spent a summer in Japan, I ate the eye of a fish because the local woman who prepared it for me asked me to eat it. She said it was healthy. Nothing in me wanted to dig that eye out of the dead fish staring up at me and swallow it, but I did it for her sake. I also learned to bow instead of hug and bring gifts when I entered a host home. Likewise, on a recent trip to Africa, I learned it was customary for the women in that area to wear long skirts or dresses. My dear friend who went with me didn't even own a skirt, yet she bought several and wore them to honor the culture we were entering.

We must judge for ourselves when it is appropriate to follow customary practices and when it is not. As we strive to be relevant, we will need the Lord's help to know where the boundary lines are, separating our freedom in Christ and sin. This doesn't mean we never seek to make changes when customs or traditions no longer fit our context or understandings. The fact that most Christian women in the world today do not cover their heads to pray reveals that at some point there was advocacy for change. The Holy Spirit helps us discern when to accept or acquiesce to traditions—for our own sake or the sake of others—and when to be used by God as an agent of reform.

What questions or issues do these three principles raise for you? Write them below. How do these questions compare to those you wrote on page 129?

Where might you turn for further study related to this passage?

Which one of the three principles stands out most to you right now, and why?

Write below any additional insights you found in this passage that you believe apply today—extending beyond lines of culture and time.

As we've learned, understanding cultural context is paramount when studying and applying Scripture so that we do not isolate verses, potentially condemning others and missing the depth of insight the Lord wants to give us. God longs to show us what He is like as we seek Him through His Word. Even as we tackle controversial topics, we can find common ground with other believers and discover truths that unite rather than divide us.

Talk with God

Invite God to show you any areas where you can grow in faith as you think through today's passage (1 Corinthians 11:1-16). Ask Him to make His Word alive and active in your life—especially the parts that are more difficult for you to understand. Pray that He would use His holy highlighter to reveal areas where He wants to encourage and challenge you with His truth—perhaps prompting you to do more study of your own.

Even as we tackle controversial topics, we can find common ground with other believers and discover truths that unite rather than divide us.

DAY 5: REMEMBERING TOGETHER

Remembering things isn't my strong suit. For the last two months I have forgotten my twins' orthodontist appointments. Eventually one of them mentioned that the rubber bands on their braces were starting to disintegrate and asked me when they were supposed to go in for a change. I hated calling to reschedule the first time because I had forgotten, so imagine my dread the next time when I realized I had missed the appointment again!

My youngest daughter has learned the secret to not missing things at the hands of her forgetful mother. She asked about her dentist appointment and wrote down the date. I'm glad she did, because I honestly would have missed it if she had not asked me to write her a note for school one day to excuse her early so that she could go to the dentist! My greatest strategy for remembering things is telling others in my family about them. We have better odds by remembering together.

God often called his people to remember important things together. Throughout Scripture we find God helping His people remember important spiritual truths through physical demonstrations. He wanted the faith community to remember together great things He had done for them, such as instituting the celebration of Passover to help the people remember God's deliverance from Egypt (Exodus 12:1-16) and observing a practice of eating bread and drinking from the cup to remember the body and blood of Christ (Luke 22:14-20).

As we complete our study of 1 Corinthians 11 today, we'll find Paul correcting the church for getting off track in their observance of the Lord's Supper or Holy Communion. Before we delve into the passage, let's take a

Extra Insight

Christ instituted the practice of Communion—often referred to as the Lord's Supper—when He ate the Passover meal with his twelve disciples (see Luke 22).

moment to read the account of Jesus instituting this practice for those who would choose to follow Him.

Read Luke 22:14-20. According to verse 19, why did Jesus say we should take the cup and the bread?

Jesus calls us to remember Him when we gather together by eating bread and drinking the fruit of the vine. Yet when we look throughout church history, we find much schism and disagreement connected to this practice that was instituted for us to remember Christ's sacrifice for us. It's easy to focus on the mode and method of Communion and forget about the heart of the matter. Restored fellowship with God through the broken body and shed blood of Christ should be the focus of our Communion gatherings.

For me, Communion is a holy moment when I gather with those in my local church to remember, reflect, and examine. I remember God's love, I reflect on the price of my salvation, and I examine my life. It is a brief but powerful moment to remember what Christ has done for me.

Now read today's passage, 1 Corinthians 11:17-34, putting a placeholder there. What problems were occurring in the Corinthian church regarding Communion?

The Corinthian church met for *agape* meals. One scholar describes the meals this way: "The Christian common meal or *agape* feast apparently followed the pattern of public sacred feasting among the Jews and Greeks. Following Greek custom, the food was brought together for all to share with the rich bringing more and the poor less."[18] But rather than sharing together, the Corinthian believers became divided. The problems that Paul identified—divisions, drunkenness, and lack of proper examination—point to a deeper root issue.

How would you describe the heart problem that these symptoms reveal? (There is not one right answer; many words could capture the essence of the Corinthians' heart problem.)

A word that came to my mind was selfishness—just plain old wanting our own way. Their heart problem also could be described as pride, greed, or arrogance. We see this sinful attitude in the believers in Corinth and in the lives of those around us, but we know it doesn't end there. I'm all too aware that I battle this issue daily. Selfishness causes me to make excuses and strive to order my life based on what is best for me. If we're honest, we must admit it's a battle we all share.

Imagine the scene in the Corinthian church. Remember that the members of this local body probably consisted of several house churches of thirty to fifty members total. The believers in these groups would have included both Jews and Gentiles. Some were influential community leaders who would have been considered rich, while others were slaves or manual laborers. Former prostitutes and idol worshipers also would have graced the tables at the *agape* meals. The people were grouping into divisions, the rich were eating what they had brought without sharing, and some impatient church members were not waiting for slaves who might have had to work late. This gives us a clearer picture of what was going on.

We are naturally drawn to people who are like us, and selfishness causes us to steer clear of those we have less in common with—especially those who might be suffering or needy.

Is there someone you have been avoiding because you approach life differently? Think of a way you can sacrificially show love to this person, and write it below:

Paul called the Corinthians to consider how their actions reflected their heart.

Read 1 Corinthians 11:22 in the margin, and underline the third of five questions Paul asked. What does this question reveal their actions were accomplishing?

This was no small matter. Paul said their actions were disgracing God's church and shaming the poor.

It's so easy to make excuses and point the finger elsewhere, but selfishness is a community-killer. In John 7:24, Jesus said, "Look beneath the surface so you can judge correctly." Paul's words to the church may seem harsh, but sometimes we need painful truth to help us course-correct, changing our path from disgrace, shame, and selfishness to remembrance.

What? Don't you have your own homes for eating and drinking? Or do you really want to disgrace God's church and shame the poor? What am I supposed to say? Do you want me to praise you? Well, I certainly will not praise you for this!
(1 Corinthians 11:22)

Just as I often forget my kids' appointments, I often forget spiritual truths. I doubt the Corinthians set out to disgrace God's church and shame the poor. It was probably a slow fade. Perhaps they decided to curb their appetite with one sip of wine and a little crumb of bread. The slippery slope toward drunkenness and disgrace likely followed on the heels of small compromises.

When and how have you seen a small compromise in your life lead to bad decisions?

As a good spiritual leader, Paul challenged the Corinthian believers to remember why they did what they did.

What two things did Paul encourage them to do? (vv. 28 and 33)

> **Communion is a time to remember Jesus and realign ourselves to the gospel that has transformed our lives.**

Paul's words to the Corinthians teach us principles that we can apply in our own lives. We need to examine ourselves and wait before approaching the Lord's Table. We must ask the hard questions and sit quietly before the Lord so that He can reveal blind spots in our lives. We honor the body and blood of Christ by allowing Communion to give us perspective and humility. When our selfishness is exposed, we then can confess and amend our ways. These are tangible ways we can get beyond ourselves!

How do these truths from God's Word challenge you in your attitude toward the Lord's Supper?

Unlike yesterday's passage where Paul's instructions were tied to customary practices, our verses today have to do with commands that transcend time and culture. The text tells us clearly to eat bread and drink from the cup to remember the body and blood of Christ, to examine ourselves while keeping an eye out for selfishness, and to wait for one another. These were not recommended practices Paul gave, telling them to judge for themselves what to do.

Communion is common ground for all believers. We can find unity without compromise as we remember the body and blood of Christ. Our focus shouldn't be whether we have individual cups or a common chalice, use wine or grape juice, or offer wafers or bread (though offering a gluten free choice can be helpful). It's not important whether we celebrate

Communion in a regular worship service or a separate gathering or observe the practice weekly, monthly, or less frequently. All of these are preferences and traditions. We may disagree about the *how*, *where*, and *when*, but we should find common ground in the *why*. Communion is a time to remember Jesus and realign ourselves to the gospel that has transformed our lives.

Talk with God

Reflect on the body and the blood of Christ, asking God to renew in your heart the depth of meaning found in the elements and expression of the Lord's Supper. Then ask the Lord to reveal any blind spots or selfishness so that you can course-correct.

Digging Deeper

As we explore "Getting Beyond Ourselves," we have to ask the question, Can Christians ever love too much? Check out the online Digging Deeper article for Week 4, "Loving Boundaries," to consider when boundaries are needed in order to live love (see AbingdonPress.com /FirstCorinthians).

WEEKLY WRAP-UP

Note: This wrap-up exercise should take you approximately 6-7 minutes for reading the chapters and a few additional minutes for recording reflections.

Take a few minutes to read 1 Corinthians 9–11 again—either out loud if possible or silently if you are in a public setting. What new insights or applications did the Holy Spirit lift off the page as you read?

Here are some of the highlights from our study this week:

- We must be willing to give up our rights for the benefit of others.
- Paul pursued common ground with others in order to spread the good news about Christ.
- Spiritual disciplines have even greater value than physical fitness because they carry over from this life to the next.
- Idolatry, immorality, and a complaining spirit can keep us focused on ourselves so that we cannot thrive in our faith or stand together for the gospel.
- We may be allowed to do anything, but we must walk closely with Jesus to discern what is beneficial.
- Getting beyond ourselves means considering the good of others over our own personal benefit.
- Even though head coverings are no longer the custom for most Christian women in the world today, we can learn valuable principles of gender interdependence from Paul's teaching.

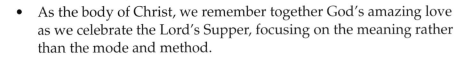

- As the body of Christ, we remember together God's amazing love as we celebrate the Lord's Supper, focusing on the meaning rather than the mode and method.

How do these themes encourage and challenge you to get beyond yourself so that you can live love toward those who are different than you?

Throughout our week of study, we've seen how the Corinthian believers grappled with their selfishness. As we close this week, my prayer is that we will continually come to the end of ourselves so that we can love others well and stand together for the gospel of Christ.

BEYOND OURSELVES

But my life is worth nothing to me unless I use it for finishing the work assigned to me by the Lord Jesus—the work of telling others the Good News about the wonderful grace of God.

(Acts 20:24)

We need to be willing to give up our _____ so that others don't stumble over the gospel.

- The root of most conflicts is unmet expectations.

- Jesus surrendered His rights for a greater purpose. (Philippians 2:3-8)

God uses us as His _____ of _____ in a world so desperately in need of it.

- Live a life filled up with love, following the example of Christ—a pleasing aroma to God. (Ephesians 5:1-2)

Finding _____ _____ is essential if we want to share the gospel with others.

- Paul looked for common ground with everyone so that he could share Jesus. (1 Corinthians 9:22-23)

This pursuit of God cannot be _____. It must include some _____ and discipline.

- We run to win an eternal prize. (1 Corinthians 9:24-27)

- God has given us everything we need for living a godly life. (2 Peter 1:3)

Week 5

LIVING LOVE

1 Corinthians 12–14

Memory Verse

Three things will last forever—faith, hope, and love—and the greatest of these is love.

(1 Corinthians 13:13)

DAY 1: OPENING PRESENTS

Living in a three-bedroom house with a husband and four kids leaves little space for clutter. My husband and I have always had a thing about excess toys, stuffed animals, and junk—especially when our kids were small. Before Christmas each year we would put a laundry basket in the center of the playroom and tell the kids they had to fill it with items to donate before we would introduce any new toys as presents. As I reflect on the years of gifts that have been exchanged in our family, I have no idea what became of most of that stuff. The gifts were expressions of love that brought temporary joy with the lasting effect of fond memories.

What is a meaningful gift you have received that you still possess?

God is a gift-giver too—but His gifts never end up in a resale shop, at the bottom of a landfill, or in a laundry basket to be donated to charity.

What do we learn about God's gifts in each of these passages?

Matthew 7:11

James 1:17

We serve a generous God who gives us good and perfect gifts! God's gifts are not only physical but also spiritual. Today as we explore 1 Corinthians 12, we will be talking about spiritual gifts. Though we do not have the original letter the Corinthians wrote to Paul asking questions, we know from 1 Corinthians 12:1 that they were interested in learning more about spiritual gifts.

Turn to 1 Corinthians 12 and put a placeholder there. According to verse 1, what was Paul's purpose in addressing the topic of spiritual gifts?

Four New Testament passages describe specific gifts that God's Spirit gives to his people. Though the lists are not exhaustive, they affirm the diverse ways God equips believers for the benefit of others.

The Corinthians had asked a question about spiritual gifts, and Paul wanted to provide clarification. Some translations say he did not want them to be uninformed or unaware.

Now read 1 Corinthians 12:2-11. Based on these verses, what do you think might have been the specific question the Corinthians asked Paul about spiritual gifts?

I wonder if they might have asked if the Spirit was the source of every gift or how they could know if someone was speaking by the Spirit.

According to verse 3, what is one indication that someone is not speaking by the Spirit of God?

In verses 4-6, Paul drives home an important principle concerning spiritual gifts. Summarize in one sentence what he was trying to communicate:

We find strong words about unity in these verses. The same God who works in my life and equips me with spiritual gifts is the same Lord who equips all Christ-followers. Yet as we look at the modern church, as well as the body of Christ throughout church history, we find much division rather than unity surrounding the topic of spiritual gifts. People argue about

- which gifts should be included in a complete list. (Romans 12, Ephesians 4, and 1 Peter 4 also discuss spiritual gifts.)
- whether all gifts are still in use today. (Some claim that a few of the gifts were in use only during the apostolic age and when the canon of Scripture was complete, those gifts ceased.)
- how gifts are to be implemented within the church. (Those with the gift of teaching can fill teaching positions while those with gifts such as faith, mercy, or discernment might serve in ways that aren't measured or clear-cut.)

These are just three examples of disunity regarding spiritual gifts.

Paul wrote to help the Corinthian believers realign to the source and purpose of their gifts. In the same way, God longs for us to recognize that while He works in different ways, He is always the same God. Hebrews 13:8 tells us that "Jesus Christ is the same yesterday, today, and forever." The Lord wants us to recognize that although we may disagree about many things regarding spiritual gifts, we shouldn't miss the bigger picture of what He is doing. God equips us with special abilities so that we might serve one another.

We can debate our varied viewpoints, but not to the extent that we fail to discover and use our own gifts.

Read 1 Corinthians 12:7. What would you say to a Christ-follower who claims that she (or he) does not possess a spiritual gift?

The text doesn't say that only mature believers receive gifts; it says that *every* Christian receives a spiritual gift from God. It is the same God who gives different gifts to different people. According to this passage, we are to use our gifts to help one another.

The Christmas gifts we've purchased for our kids over the years were for their own personal enjoyment. They played with plastic dishes, rammed remote control cars into the couch, and wore clothes and shoes that they desired. But the spiritual gifts that God gives are not meant to make us feel good—though they certainly do. They are meant to edify and build up others in the body. And every gift is important.

Look back at 1 Corinthians 12:8-11 and list the gifts mentioned:

First Corinthians gives us the most complete list of spiritual gifts to be found in any passage of Scripture.

Read Romans 12:6-8, Ephesians 4:11, and 1 Peter 4:10-11 and record below any gifts named in these passages that are not found in 1 Corinthians 12:8-11 (which you listed above):

What additional insights did you glean from these passages regarding spiritual gifts?

Recognizing that people use different terms and definitions for the gifts found in the four main Scripture passages that mention spiritual gifts, here is a compilation of the gifts:

Administration	Leadership
Apostleship	Mercy/Compassion
Discernment	Miracles
Evangelism	Pastor/Shepherd
Exhortation/Encouragement	Prophecy
Faith	Serving/Ministering
Giving	Teaching
Healing	Tongues
Interpretation of Tongues	Wisdom
Knowledge	

Discovering our gifts can help us understand how God wants to use us to build up the rest of the body. One helpful tool in the process of discovery is a spiritual gifts inventory or survey. There are a number of different inventories that ask a series of questions and then give a score for each area of giftedness. By identifying areas where we score higher, we can further investigate or confirm the hunches we might already have about which gifts God has entrusted to us. For more detailed descriptions of the gifts and to take a survey, see www.ministrymatters.com/spiritualgifts (set up a free account and then take the survey), www.spiritualgiftstest.com/test/adult, or another online spiritual gifts inventory. (You might find it helpful to take more than one survey and compare the results.)

As you look over the list of gifts above, which two would you say might be gifts God has given you? (After taking a gifts inventory—whether in the past, now, or later—do the results confirm that either of these gifts might be yours?)

Circle the gift above that you believe might be your primary or strongest gift. If you're not sure, simply choose one of the gifts. What are some ways you have used this gift for the benefit of the body of Christ?

Rather than getting caught up in disagreements about the gifts, we should devote our time to discovering and using our own gifts.

According to 1 Corinthians 12:11, who decides which gift each person should have?

The Holy Spirit chooses our gifts. Our responsibility is to discover and use them, recognizing God as their source.

From a young age I have loved to study and explain things. My shyness prevented me from teaching in front of large groups until recent years. I felt comfortable teaching children in Sunday school or leading a small Bible study, but God has continued to stretch and grow me to use my gift even when I am uncomfortable. I don't always look forward to preparing and teaching, but once I begin, I feel energized. Even now I sometimes dread when it is my turn to teach the middle school youth group, yet as I study the lesson and then begin to teach the students, I feel God's pleasure. I know that teaching is a gift God has given me. My responsibility is to use this gift how He directs me, even when I'm scared or tired or lazy.

Refer to the gift you circled and describe a time when you felt God enabling you as you implemented the gift:

God gives us the gifts and empowers us to use them by His Holy Spirit for the benefit of one another. Alongside the descriptions of spiritual gifts we find in Romans 12, Ephesians 4, and 1 Peter 4, we read of the need for unity or harmony. (And as we will see in tomorrow's lesson, Paul also writes about unity using the analogy of the human body.)

Read the verses below and circle any words related to unity or harmony:

Live in harmony with each other. Don't be too proud to enjoy the company of ordinary people. And don't think you know it all!

(Romans 12:16)

Make every effort to keep yourselves united in the Spirit, binding yourselves together with peace. For there is one body and one Spirit, just as you have been called to one glorious hope for the future.

(Ephesians 4:3-4)

Most important of all, continue to show deep love for each other, for love covers a multitude of sins.

(1 Peter 4:8)

God knows us so well. He understood that in response to the distribution of different abilities, our flesh would be tempted to compare, criticize, or puff up with spiritual pride. Just as I've watched my children on Christmas morning desire their siblings' gifts or express discontent with their own gifts, we can demonstrate the same behavior when it comes to spiritual gifts. So in these teachings on gifts, our Lord lovingly warns us to live in harmony.

In closing, I'd like to highlight four universal principles that we've explored in our study today in 1 Corinthians 12:

- God gives different kinds of spiritual gifts. (v. 4)
- The Holy Spirit is the source of all gifts and decides which gift each person should have. (vv. 4 and 11)
- A spiritual gift is given to every believer. (v. 7)
- Spiritual gifts are given so that we can help one another. (v. 7)

As you review these principles, put a star by the one that stands out to you personally. Briefly explain below why this principle resonates with you:

> **God gives us the gifts and empowers us to use them by His Holy Spirit for the benefit of one another.**

Though we love to give gifts, God is the ultimate gift giver! He graciously and generously gives us gifts that yield eternal results as we use them for the benefit of others. May you revel in the gifts He has given you and feel His pleasure as you put your gifts into action serving others!

Talk with God

If you aren't sure what your spiritual gift is, take some time now to pray and ask God to reveal it to you (or you may have more than one). Consider areas of strength and enjoyment in the various areas listed on page 146, feedback and affirmation you've received from others, and results from spiritual gifts inventories you have taken. If you know your gift(s), talk with God about how you are using your gift(s). Pray for new opportunities to build up the body of Christ in your sphere of influence.

DAY 2: HEAD, SHOULDERS, KNEES, AND TOES

Last summer my daughter and I were invited to attend a camp for teen girls with alopecia and their mothers. The organization Locks of Love, which provides hairpieces for children who have lost their hair due to alopecia or cancer, hosted this getaway for education and support. My daughter was able to meet other girls her age who also struggle with things such as wearing wigs, going to sleepovers, and having no eyelashes.

As we listened to an expert in the field share about recent medical advances, we learned more about immune privilege, hair follicles, and T cells. I sat in awe as I heard how scientists can disrupt communication between the immune attackers and healthy cells. I never knew that the body has JAK 1, 2, and 3 systems that can be inhibited with certain medications. Although none of the developments are right for my daughter, I sat there questioning how anyone could learn about the intricacies of the human body and not believe in a Master Designer. All that must happen for us to see and smell and walk and produce hair reveals an amazing Creator!

Just as God designed the systems of our bodies to work together in unison, so He created the church to function with unity in the midst of diversity. In the last portion of 1 Corinthians 12, Paul further expounds on spiritual gifts using the human body as an illustration of different parts working together for a common purpose.

Turn to 1 Corinthians 12:12-31 and put a placeholder there. List below some of the different backgrounds of the Corinthian believers mentioned in verse 13:

The Corinthian church was multicultural, socioeconomically diverse, and inclusive of men and women who were slaves as well as those who were free. Some of the believers had been devout Jews and others had been idol worshipers or prostitutes. This variety sounds wonderful to us because diversity is something we strive for in the church today.

What are some of the different backgrounds you see in your church and/or other church bodies in your area?

The church I attend includes former drug addicts and alcoholics as well as those who have ongoing personal battles. Some people have come from extremely conservative religious traditions while others had no religious instruction at all. We have people who are barely making ends meet and others who have prestigious jobs with high incomes. In addition, there is diversity in age groups, personality types, birth order, love languages, and spiritual gifts—just to name a few of our differences.

What are some disagreements or problems you have seen among believers because of differences?

Extra Insight

"In all three of the 'body' passages of Paul's letters, there is an emphasis on love.... It has well been said that love is the 'circulatory system' of the body of Christ."[1]

Sometimes we can forget that everyone isn't like us. We forget that others do not have the same struggles, gifts, or personalities we have. A woman who is an extrovert may not understand why another woman avoids big women's events and prefers smaller gatherings. A person with the gift of mercy might judge others for not spending time with those who are hurting while another with the gift of helps can't understand why everyone else in her Bible study group isn't motivated to take a meal to someone who just had a baby. God gave us specific gifts to help others in different ways, but He knows that in our flesh we can become self-righteous and judgmental.

On the flip side of our tendency to judge others is our struggle with inferiority. Some of us look around and see the extroverts who are the life of the party and the host who has the gift of hospitality, and we feel less than. Paul addressed the issues of comparison and inferiority in his words to the Corinthians.

Read 1 Corinthians 12:14-17. In the speech bubbles to the left, write the hypothetical words of the ear and the foot.

We may laugh at the thought of an ear wanting to be an eye or a foot wishing it were a hand, but the concept hits all too close to home.

When have you wished you were more like someone else, and why?

Many times I have longed for the creativity of others—from decorating their homes to coordinating their accessories. Others exercise great faith while I seem to continually work mine out, chasing away doubt. It's easy to fix our eyes on others and, consequently, fail to appreciate and use the gifts we have been given. Longing for a gift the Lord hasn't given me communicates my lack of trust in His decisions.

Write 1 Corinthians 12:18 below:

> It's easy to fix our eyes on others and, consequently, fail to appreciate and use the gifts we have been given.

God puts each part just where He wants it! As the Master Designer, He calls us to expend our time, talents, and treasures using what He has given us—rather than wanting and wishing for something different. We are not carbon copies. God made us uniquely, intricately, and purposefully.

Take a moment to describe some of the unique qualities God has created in you. You may choose to list spiritual gifts, temperament qualities, love languages, personality traits, talents, or other special abilities that God has given you. (Remember: It isn't prideful to acknowledge what God has given you any more than it is prideful for an eye to acknowledge that it can see!)

Now choose one of these things, and write it in the blanks below:

The Lord has given me the special ability to _____

_____, and I will use this to help others by _____

_____.

When our eyes are focused on what we believe is *superior* or *inferior*, we are distracted from allowing God to use us. Some gifts may seem to be showier than others, but Paul told the Corinthians that some of the gifts we regard as less honorable are those we should clothe with great care. In verses 25-26, we again find the theme of unity in the midst of diversity: "This makes for harmony among the members, so that all the members care for each other. If one part suffers, all the parts suffer with it, and if one part is honored, all the parts are glad." Rather than comparing and competing, we are called to help one another!

In a sense, my daughter's alopecia is a mutiny within her body. Her immune system was designed to protect her body against foreign invaders, yet somehow her hair follicles have lost the immune privilege that keeps them from being attacked. Her own body is destroying something that is supposed to be there. If we're not careful, we can do that within the body of Christ. We must stop seeking uniformity and learn to embrace unity instead.

How sad it would be to have churches that are full of "eyes" with all the "ears" meeting across town. God wants us to work together, using our gifts to help one another. Just as the human body was designed to compensate when one area is weak, we too should help—rather than criticize—those who are struggling to use their gifts.

In 1 Corinthians 12, I see God calling us to

- admit that we are different.
- recognize that the same God equips us differently.
- focus on our gifts and callings instead of comparing ourselves to others.
- trust that God has given us the best gifts for us, rather than wish we had other gifts.
- give others the benefit of the doubt, rather than criticism, when they function differently than we do.

Write a short prayer below asking God to help you live out these biblical truths as you use your gifts to encourage and help others:

What is one truth from today's lesson that stands out to you?

> **God colors outside the lines and wants us to be dependent on Him, listening for the unique ways He will use our abilities.**

At a recent women's retreat, a few of us were talking about spiritual gifts. One woman mentioned that she doesn't know how her gift fits in at our church. Someone spoke up and said that *we* are the church! She can use her gift however the Lord leads, even if that doesn't directly fit with our list of volunteer needs and opportunities. One woman shared that God led her to start a playgroup in her neighborhood. She was using her gift of hospitality in a way not officially connected to the church. Another gal shared that she exercised her gift of administration by running a nonprofit that serves the underprivileged in our community. Her role as a church greeter isn't as connected to her spiritual gift as her ministry outside the church is.

We often want everything to fit into neat boxes, but God's ways and our ways aren't always the same. When it comes to spiritual gifts, we need to accept that God colors outside the lines and wants us to be dependent on Him, listening for the unique ways He will use our abilities. As we listen, let's ask the Lord to help us achieve harmony in the midst of our differences.

Talk with God

Spend a few moments praying for your church, asking God to give you a renewed sense of the importance of working in harmony for the gospel. Pray for your leaders to guide your members in using your gifts so that you function as a healthy body.

DAY 3: THE GREATEST OF THESE

We have finally come to the best known and most loved chapter in Paul's first letter to the Corinthians—the love chapter. You've likely heard this passage read at a wedding—perhaps even your own. When we think of love, our minds often conjure up images of romance novels or chick flicks. Yet as we've studied the letter that Paul wrote to the church in Corinth, we've found that the original audience wasn't involved in a gushy love story. In fact, they were a group of people struggling to get along. Realigning ourselves with God's definition of love is important as we commit our lives to another person in marriage, but it becomes critical when we are struggling to get along because of our differences.

As the body of Christ, we need to remember in the midst of our trials and conflicts how God explains love. That is the context of today's passage. Before we jump into the love chapter, let's check out 1 John 4:7-12 to discover the source of this love.

Read 1 John 4:7-12 and answer the following questions:

Where does love come from? (v. 7)

Who is love? (v. 8)

How did God demonstrate His love for us? (v. 9)

What is real love? (v. 10)

How do we express God's love? (vv. 11-12)

As we lift the lid on 1 Corinthians 13 and read of a love that seems unattainable for us, let us be encouraged by the reminder that this perfect love cannot be found by looking inward. God is love, and our relationship with Him is our source of love.

Extra Insight

Three different Greek words translated as "love" are *eros* (romantic love), *phileo* (brotherly love), and *agape* (supernatural, godly love). Two of these words, *phileo* and *agape*, are found in the New Testament.[2] *Agape* is the word used in 1 Corinthians 13.

Turn to 1 Corinthians 13 and put a placeholder there. Read verses 1-3, and then put a check mark beside the example Paul mentioned that you think would be the most impressive to include on your resumé:

__ Speaking all the languages of the earth

__ Understanding all God's secret plans

__ Possessing all knowledge

__ Having faith that can move mountains

__ Giving everything you own to the poor

__ Sacrificing your body

I can't even wrap my mind around speaking another language, much less all of them! To know all of God's secret plans or be able to literally move mountains seems like something out of a superhero movie. Yet what does God say these great things are without love? Yep, nothing! Zip. Zero. Without love, nothing of real value can be gained.

When and how have you experienced the truth that a lack of love drains the value from a possession, talent, gift, or relationship?

Paul didn't want the believers in Corinth—who were squabbling over leaders, lawsuits, immorality, idolatry, and spiritual gifts—to miss the big picture of what is most important in God's economy. He called them to love above all else. As believers, we are called to do the same. Even when we are doing good things, we can lose the love behind the actions if we do not continually depend on God.

What are some things you know God has called you to do in this season of life?

> **Even when we are doing good things, we can lose the love behind the actions if we do not continually depend on God.**

While our lists may not include moving mountains or speaking every language, we care for our families, work hard at our jobs, and give ourselves in ministry to others. We may begin activities with loving intentions, but our love can grow cold if we drift away from intimacy with God. Remember that good beginnings don't guarantee good endings. We must stay connected with Jesus so that He can infuse us continually with His love. God is love. When we drift into self-reliance, love begins to wane.

Choose two of the things you listed previously, and write each in a sentence below (I did one as an example):

If I teach Sunday school but don't do it out of the overflow of God's love in me, it means nothing.

If I _____ but don't do it out of the overflow of God's love in me, it means _____ .

If I _____ but don't do it out of the overflow of God's love in me, it will result in _____ .

Whether I am cleaning my house or leading a Bible study, I know the difference between doing it because I have to get it done and doing it for God's glory. I feel the difference in my attitude, words, and level of joy. Though the toilets may still shine when I clean with the wrong attitude, on Judgment Day that work will burn up like wood, hay, and straw. However, when I do even the most menial task out of the overflow of God's love in my life, I know that my work will pass the test of fire.

Because love is the greatest, God used Paul's pen to give us an in-depth description so that we will be clear about what love looks like when fleshed out in real life.

Read 1 Corinthians 13:4-8, and fill in the chart below to tell what love is and is not:

Love Is	Love Is Not
v. 4	v. 4
v. 4	v. 4
v. 6	v. 4
v. 7	v. 5
v. 7	v. 5
v. 7	v. 5
v. 7	v. 5
v. 8 Never Failing!	v. 6

Extra Insight

"A characteristic of Gentile worship, especially the worship of the Greek god of wine, Dionysus, and of the goddess Cybele, was the clanging of cymbals and the blaring of trumpets."[3]

As you consider God's call to love others with this kind of love, in what areas of your life do you sense God speaking a word of affirmation or encouragement? Now, in what areas do you sense the conviction of the Holy Spirit?

Areas of Affirmation/Encouragement   Areas of Conviction

The idea of love not being irritable stands out to me. Sometimes I can be moody and grumpy toward those closest to me. Patience is also a good litmus test in my life. When I find myself growing impatient, I know I need to get in God's presence and soak up more of His patient love.

The text also says that love does not keep a record of wrongs—in other words, it does not store the memory of being wronged. This one can be tough for all of us! One scholar wrote, "The word translated as *store up* (*logizesthai*) is an accountant's word. It is the word used for entering up an item in a ledger so that it will not be forgotten."[4] To love like God, we should not hold on to the wrongs done to us.

This is easier said than done.

Anytime we find ourselves being rude—whether we're on the phone with a telemarketer or posting a comment online—we are not living love. I heard someone use the term "keyboard courage" to refer to comments people post online that they would never say in person. Before our fingers react on social media, we should consider whether our words overflow from love. We can speak truth boldly, but never rudely. This is hard.

We can become so stuck on being right that we forget love is the greatest. Jesus showed love, and it flew in the face of many religious leaders who were so focused on rules that they lost the wonder of a relationship with God.

At summer camp when I was a teen, a teacher challenged us to read one chapter in the Gospels each night before bed. I started with Matthew and made my way to the end of John. I'll never forget being so amazed by the grace and love of Jesus in those pages. As I read about His encounters with a man he healed on the Sabbath, a woman he met at a well, and a woman caught in adultery, I began to wonder if the church resembled the Pharisees more than our Lord.

In his commentary on 1 Corinthians, William Barclay wrote, "So many good church people would have sided with the rulers and not with Jesus if they had had to deal with the woman taken in adultery."[5] I fear he might be right. Jesus broke the letter of the law to fulfill the spirit of the law.

When has your passion for truth resulted in words or actions that are unloving according to 1 Corinthians 13?

Read Mark 12:28-31. How does Jesus' answer regarding the greatest commandment support Paul's teaching about the importance of love?

When we disagree, God calls us to approach each other with His love. We may not see an issue the same way, but we can learn to treat each other with love in the process of dialogue. At the end of chapter 13, we find a key to showing love when we disagree.

Read 1 Corinthians 13:9-12. What does verse 9 say about our knowledge?

What illustration does Paul use in verse 12 to describe our imperfect vision?

On the heels of his discussion of love, Paul described our incomplete and imperfect view. Knowing that I often struggle to understand what God is doing in my own heart and life, I certainly cannot pretend to have a grasp on what He is doing in the lives of others. Recognizing that I don't have all the answers motivates me to treat others with love.

I might disagree on a nonessential point of theology with you, but why would I treat you unkindly, impatiently, or rudely when it's possible that, in the end, I might be wrong? My view is partial and incomplete. I am prayerfully seeking God, studying His Word, and seeking wise counsel to make decisions in my life. Yet at the end of the day, my knowledge is incomplete. Since I cannot fully understand my own puzzling life, I should be gracious and loving toward those with whom I disagree.

How does recognizing that your own knowledge is partial and incomplete motivate you to be more gracious toward someone you currently disagree with?

> **Recognizing that I don't have all the answers motivates me to treat others with love.**

Maturity has been a theme throughout the Corinthian letter. We saw in chapter 2 that Paul called the church spiritual babies who needed milk. He also said that their quarrels revealed their immaturity.

Read 1 Corinthians 13:11. What did Paul imply about children?

How would you describe the differences between the thoughts, words, and reasoning abilities of children and adults?

Extra Insight

"Corinth was famous for its manufacture of mirrors. But the modern mirror as we know it, with its perfect reflection, did not emerge until the thirteenth century. The Corinthian mirror was made of highly polished metal and, even at its best, gave but an imperfect reflection."[6]

Paul reminded the Corinthians that children speak, reason, and think differently than adults.

With time and maturity, people grow to be more focused on the needs of others than their own needs. Mature adults also tend to care less about the fleeting pleasures of life and more about lasting joy. With maturity comes an emphasis on relationships over possessions, the ability to resolve conflict more respectfully, and the realization that diplomacy and listening are more effective than wrestling matches.

All of my kids went through biting, hitting, and scratching phases. Thankfully, with time and maturity, they are no longer using their teeth and nails to try to get their way. Paul longed for the Corinthians to put away their childish pursuits and stop elevating certain leaders, fighting over possessions, and comparing their spiritual gifts. He called them to grow up and realize that love is more important than getting your way.

Because of our partial understanding, we can disagree, discuss, and seek to learn from one another, but we should do it with maturity—no rudeness, name-calling, boasting, jealousy, or demands. Love celebrates truth winning out. Love isn't a cop-out, throwing truth out the window. We still stand on the truth of God's Word without compromise. However, we must be careful to navigate gray areas with love and humility.

It's important to understand that love and approval are two very different things. I can love someone deeply and at the same time disapprove of his or her choices. God is love. He always loves me, but He doesn't approve of everything I do, say, or think. In fact, He lovingly calls me to turn from my sin because He knows it will not lead to blessing in my life. So as we follow God, we too can love others freely without approving of everything they do.

I've watched a friend struggle with this very issue as her young adult daughter began making choices contrary to her Christian faith. Of course, this momma loves her daughter dearly, but she doesn't want to communicate her approval of unbiblical behaviors.

What advice would you give to this mother?

The line between enabling bad choices and showing unfailing love can be tough to navigate. We need the help of the Holy Spirit and the reminder that our view is partial and incomplete in order to err on the side of love without enabling others in bad behavior or developing codependent relationships. As my wise friend Mary Beth pointed out, "You can be a blessing without giving your blessing." Loving, giving, and serving others do not equate with condoning all of someone's life choices.

Consider a complicated or challenging relationship in your life. What are some practical ways you can show love without giving approval in areas of disagreement?

"You can be
a blessing
without giving
your blessing."
—Mary Beth

We do not have to compromise our beliefs in order to show love to others. Instead, we can respectfully share our views and display God's kindness and patience as we dialogue with maturity. To do this, we must remember these truths from 1 Corinthians 13:

- Love comes from God.
- To show God's love to those around us, we must stay close to God.
- Love is greater than any talent or ability.
- Without love, our words and actions mean nothing.
- Love is patient, kind, humble, forgiving, truthful, persevering, faithful, hopeful, and enduring.
- Our view of life is partial and incomplete.
- Love and approval are two different things.

Star two of these truths that stand out to you personally. Now, write the last verse of chapter 13 below:

God's Word tells us to pursue eternal things, and 1 Corinthians 13:13 reminds us that faith, hope, and love will last forever—"and the greatest of these is love." Because God is love, embracing the love that Jesus has for us empowers us to extend His love to those around us. In all that we do today, tomorrow, and the days to come, let's remember that the greatest thing we can do is love and be loved!

The greatest
thing we can
do is love and
be loved!

Talk with God

Reread 1 Corinthians 13:4-7, replacing the word *love* with the name *Jesus*. Then say a prayer thanking Jesus for His love for you. Ask Him to help you love others in your life with His love and grace.

DAY 4: PURSUING LOVE IN REAL-LIFE SITUATIONS

I know and respect Christians who hold different views on the gift of tongues. Some believe it is a valid gift today while others believe it was given for a specific time and purpose and is no longer in use. Some believe it involves speaking in foreign languages while others believe it includes ecstatic utterances. When it comes to the gift of tongues, we tend to have many beliefs and questions. Rather than unpacking that here, I invite you to read the Digging Deeper article "Controversial Gifts" (see the note in the margin). For our focus today, I'm excited for us to look at the gift of tongues in a way that will bring unity as we discover some universal truths we all can apply.

On the heels of 1 Corinthians 13, which is about love and our incomplete view of life, the last thing I believe the Lord would want us to do is argue over the semantics of one of the spiritual gifts. In fact, Paul basically said that the Corinthian believers' root problem in regard to their use of the gift of tongues was a lack of love.

> **Think about a current relational conflict of your own. How might a lack of love be at the root of the problem?**

We can learn some relevant truths from the Corinthian believers' lack of love so that we can guard against falling into a similar trap.

> **Turn to 1 Corinthians 14 and put a placeholder there. Read verse 1 and circle below how your Bible translation describes what you should do related to love:**
>
> **Let love be your highest goal/greatest aim (NLT, TLB)**
>
> **Follow the way of love (NIV)**
>
> **Follow after charity (KJV)**
>
> **Go after a life of love (MSG)**
>
> **Pursue love (CEB, ESV, HCSB, NASB, NKJV, NRSV)**
>
> **You should seek after love (NCV)**

Digging Deeper

Much disagreement surrounds the spiritual gift of tongues. Check out one of two online Digging Deeper articles for Week 5, "A Controversial Gift," to gain some clarity about three common views regarding this gift (see AbingdonPress.com /FirstCorinthians).

When Paul called the Corinthians to pursue love in verse 1, he used the Greek word *dioko,* which means "to follow, hunt, or chase after with intensity."[7] Then, in the same verse, he used a lesser verb to say that we should *desire* spiritual gifts. Paul went on to caution the Corinthian believers concerning their lack of love in three areas. Let's look at each one together.

1. Valuing one gift over another.

Paul didn't teach against the practice of speaking in tongues. In fact, he said in verse 18 that he possessed the gift of tongues. Although this was Paul's own gift, given by the Spirit (1 Corinthians 12:11), he made a case that the church was out of balance in its focus on the gift of tongues. Paul didn't want to squelch the spontaneity of the Spirit's leading among the Corinthians but hoped to restore order in their meetings.

As we consider our own extremes related to overemphasizing certain aspects of our faith, we too need to evaluate and make changes where we lack balance. Too much of a good thing can be a danger.

I confess that when I had my first child, I was a total health nut. My son didn't taste sugar until he ate cake on his first birthday, and I juiced organic apples and carrots for him every day during his first three years. (Remember, I didn't have any other children at the time and clearly had too much time on my hands!) Then one day I noticed that my very pale-skinned boy looked like he had a tan in the middle of winter. A kind friend told me I had given him so much carrot juice that he was literally turning orange. She said it wouldn't hurt him but I might want to tone it down. Who knew you could overdo carrot juice? Clearly not me!

When I am in the middle of a writing project, my housekeeping suffers. In certain seasons of life, my husband and I have so overscheduled our lives with ministry engagements that we have neglected our marriage and parenting. All of us can struggle to find and maintain balance. We can become so focused on our physical health that we neglect our spiritual disciplines. On the flip side, we can be spiritually fit but need to get moving physically. Thankfully, when we get off track our loving God calls us back to a place of balance.

Paul warned the Corinthians that an excessive focus on one thing can lead to the neglect of other important things.

Reread verse 1. Which gift did Paul say needed to be more prominent in the Corinthians' assemblies?

How would you define the gift of prophecy?

Extra Insight

Glossolalia is the Greek word for speaking in tongues.[8]

An excessive focus on one thing can lead to the neglect of other important things.

So then faith comes by hearing, and hearing by the word of God.
(Romans 10:17 NKJV)

The prophets in the Old Testament spoke God's messages. Sometimes they proclaimed future events by *foretelling* and other times they taught truths about God by *forthtelling*. Given Paul's concern here for the Corinthians to hear sound teaching, we know that Paul was referring to the latter kind of prophecy—forthtelling. One scholar writes, "Paul does not think of prophecy as predicting future events; instead its purpose is to address the hearts of the hearers and to encourage them in the faith."[9] Because of their emphasis on speaking in tongues that people could not understand, the Corinthians' meetings lacked adequate proclamation of God's truth.

Read Romans 10:17 in the margin. How does faith come?

In order for the early church members to grow in faith and knowledge, they needed to hear the Word of God taught rather than listen to unknown languages without an interpreter.

According to 1 Corinthians 14:3, what are three benefits of speaking prophecy in the church?

1.

2.

3.

Paul knew that prophecy had the power to strengthen, encourage, and comfort the body of Christ. He wanted these believers who lived in the midst of a pagan culture to hear sound teaching that would realign them to God's truth and uplift them. So he admonished the church for giving too much floor time to the gift of tongues and not enough to the clear teaching of God's Word.

How have you seen a group or individual overconcentrate on one aspect of Christianity?

Now let's bring it a little closer to home. Where in your faith or life do you lack balance right now?

> **Whether it comes to our health, relationships, theology, or time management, we can pursue love by evaluating ourselves to see where we might be off balance.**

Write a prayer below asking God to help you achieve balance in this area. If you couldn't think of anything, write a prayer asking God to search your heart and reveal any area that might need attention.

Some of us may need to relax a regimented routine, and others of us may need to get on a schedule. Maybe we need to pull away from spending so much time online and find practical ways to serve others. Whether it comes to our health, relationships, theology, or time management, we can pursue love by evaluating ourselves to see where we might be off balance.

2. Focusing on self instead of edifying others.

A second warning Paul gave had to do with self-absorption. We learn from one scholar that the pagan cults in Corinth also practiced speaking in tongues: "Various Greco-Roman religions were well-known for their outbursts of ecstatic speech and unintelligible repetition of 'nonsense' syllables. This is precisely what Paul wanted to avoid."[10] Once again Paul was calling the church to be different from the world around them, cautioning them not to look for a divine "high" for their own good as the pagans did.

According to 1 Corinthians 12:7, the purpose of spiritual gifts is to help one another. Here in chapter 14 Paul was reminding the church to edify others with their gifts rather than seek attention or personal fulfillment. This reminder echoed the earlier theme of giving up rights for the sake of others. The Corinthians could not have missed Paul's call to build one another up rather than seek personal gratification. Narcissism is a love killer. God calls us to use our gifts for His glory and for the benefit of others.

When it comes to serving in the church, we can start out with selfless motives and slowly shift toward a self-serving focus without even realizing it. We can fall into the habit of serving to win the applause of others or to feel good about ourselves.

Write below some of the ways you serve (whether in your home, church, workplace, or community). Then ask God to renew in you a pure motivation of love for others. If you choose, write your prayer in the margin.

> We can fall into the habit of serving to win the applause of others or to feel good about ourselves.

3. Lacking relevance.

Paul pointed out that worship should be understandable. He said the church shouldn't forbid a gift that God clearly ordained but should seek to use it in a way that edifies.

Read 1 Corinthians 14:7-11. What are three ways Paul illustrated the need for intelligibility?

Verse	Illustration
7	
8	
10-11	

What key message is Paul communicating with these examples?

Now read 1 Corinthians 14:20. What kind of thinking did Paul imply that the Corinthian believers were practicing in regard to the gift of tongues?

What did Paul say in verse 23 that unbelievers might think if they saw the Corinthian believers speaking in tongues?

Once again Paul was calling the Corinthians childish—this time because of their overemphasis on speaking in tongues. Just as parents long for their children to grow up, Paul instructed the church to recognize that their unintelligible practices were not reaching those in their midst—neither believers nor unbelievers. In order for believers to grow and unbelievers to be convicted of sin, both groups needed to hear the Word of God taught clearly.

Paul cautioned that visitors who came to a church gathering and observed the believers speaking in tongues might think that they were just another pagan cult full of emotional experience. He was not saying that unbelievers would think the believers were crazy, as a literal reading of

English translations of verse 23 might suggest. Rather, as one commentator explains it, "The typical pagan Corinthian observing such a scene would say, 'Oh, this is just another group like the devotees of Dionysus or Cybele'—one more consumer option in a pluralistic religious market."[11] Paul reminded the Corinthians of the power of the intelligible words of the gospel and compelled them to preach God's Word so that those far from God might encounter the truth and be forever changed.

As believers, we can embrace the importance of the teaching and preaching of God's Word so that we can grow in faith and those far from God can come to know Him. Unlike the Corinthians, we have quick and easy access to God's Word. We can read our own copies of the Bible; attend a variety of worship services; access sermons and Bible teaching via podcasts, downloads, or streaming video; and participate in Bible studies in person and online. We then can share the truths we learn with others in ways that are relevant and understandable to them.

What is something God has been teaching you that you would like to share with one or more persons in your life (think kids, grandkids, neighbors, coworkers, friends, or people you disciple or mentor)?

How can you share it in a way that will be relevant to this person or persons?

Paul instructed the Corinthians to pursue love in real-life situations. In what current circumstance is the Lord calling you to follow or chase after love with great intensity?

Regardless of our beliefs and questions related to the gift of tongues, we all can agree to pursue love as we discuss and live out the gifts God has given us, remembering that love is the greatest (1 Corinthians 13:13). We can learn to live with ambiguity in some areas, acknowledging that now we know in part but one day we will see everything with perfect clarity (1 Corinthians 13:12). Until that day comes, let us love one another well and seek to build one another up—even when we disagree.

We can learn to live with ambiguity in some areas, acknowledging that now we know in part but one day we will see everything with perfect clarity.

Talk with God

Spend some time reflecting on today's passage, 1 Corinthians 14:1-25. Ask God to show you how you can pursue love with greater intensity this week. Continue to pray that God will develop your spiritual gifts for the benefit of others.

DAY 5: SOLUTION-ORIENTED

Life can seem pointless and even annoying at times. When I remember that God has a plan for the future, it changes my perspective on things that seem mundane in the moment. The early Christians adopted an apocalyptic worldview. They believed Jesus was coming back soon. Paul wrote about the return of Christ often in his letters. Realizing that God has a master plan with a good ending in which justice and mercy reign helps us change our attitude when life is confusing.

Today we'll find that Paul provided a solution-oriented approach to the problems we looked at yesterday. Rather than just telling the Corinthians what they were doing wrong, Paul laid out steps to correct the problem.

What is a problem you are currently facing?

Although today's passage may not lay out specific steps for your particular issue, I pray that you will be motivated to seek God for the next right thing He might call you to do. Let's see what directions Paul gave the Corinthians.

Read 1 Corinthians 14:26-40, putting a placeholder there. What is something we learn about God's character in verse 33?

It gives me great comfort to know that our God is not a God of confusion or disorder. He is a God of peace.

Does having things in order typically bring you peace? Why or why not?

When the dishes are done, the bills are paid, or deadlines are met, I feel peace. In contrast, I lack peace when tasks go unfinished for too long or my priorities get out of order. Likewise, even when I don't understand His plans or ways, I can be confident that our God is a God of order and peace who always knows what He is doing.

Look up the following verses and write what you learn about God:

Isaiah 55:8-9

Psalm 85:8

Acts 10:36

Philippians 4:7

In many places in Scripture, we see order in God's character. He is not a God of confusion or chaos.

Read James 3:13-18. According to these verses, what kind of forces are at the heart of disorder?

James tells us that disorder is earthly, unspiritual, and demonic. Knowing that our God is a God of order, Paul laid out some practical ways to bring order to the church services in Corinth.

According to 1 Corinthians 14:26, what were some of the elements included in the meetings of the church?

What was the goal of all these parts of the service?

Paul reminded them again that the objective was the strengthening of everyone. Earlier in the chapter he had used the Greek word for edification (*oikodome*), which literally means "housebuilding."[13] When a building is being constructed, an architect designs blueprints and works out the best use of space. Likewise, our God calls us to construct a plan so that we might strengthen and encourage one another. When we recognize that we are not building one another up, we need the wisdom of the Holy Spirit to set guidelines and get back on track. Paul did just that.

Extra Insight

"Keep in mind that the members of the Corinthian church did not sit in the services with Bible in their laps. The New Testament was being written, and the Old Testament scrolls were expensive and not available to most believers."[14]

Fill in the following chart according to Paul's directives in verses 27-31:

Verse	Guideline
27a	No more than . . .
27b	They must speak . . .
27c	Someone must . . .
28	If no one can interpret . . .
29a	Let two or three . . .
29b	Let others . . .
30-31	They should . . .

Sometimes love requires a plan. Putting a plan in action can bring order where there is disorder.

How have you seen a plan bring order to a church service, an organization, or a relationship?

*¹⁹ "Do not stifle the Holy Spirit. ²⁰ Do not scoff at prophecies, ²¹ but test everything that is said. Hold on to what is good."
(1 Thessalonians 5:19-21)*

One of the things Paul instructed the Corinthians to do was evaluate what is said (v. 29b).

Read 1 Thessalonians 5:19-21 in the margin. How do Paul's words to the church in Thessalonica resemble his admonition to the church in Corinth?

How can you apply these commands to your own reading or hearing of God's Word? What are some practical ways to "test everything" and "hold on to what is good"?

My parents trained me and my siblings to be critical thinkers. I err on the side of questioning everything. Sometimes it hurts my head. Every sermon I hear (even those preached by my husband) finds me asking questions such as, "Is that statement true, and does it fit with the whole of Scripture?" and "Was that passage properly interpreted and applied?" The danger for me is that by focusing so intently on testing the message, I might miss what the Spirit is trying to say to me. We need balance as we seek to evaluate what is being said while listening for what the Holy Spirit is speaking to us. This requires active listening and evaluation as we hear God's messages presented.

When I was in high school, my pastor would comment about the scowl on my face as he taught. I assured him that was only my thinking face. Now as I teach, I recognize the "thinking face" on those who are listening and testing as they should.

According to the following passages, why must we evaluate the teaching we hear?

2 Peter 2:1

1 John 4:1

Like the Corinthian believers, we too must test the messages we hear because many false prophets twist lies with the truth.

What can help you discern the difference between true and false teaching?

The more we know and study God's powerful Word, the better we will become at spotting a fake. When we hear teaching that doesn't sit well in our spirits, we must pray, search the Scriptures, and seek wise counsel from others to discern whether the message is incongruent with God's Word or if we might be experiencing personal conviction.

What are some ways you can implement a solution-oriented plan to study God's Word with greater passion?

Remember that people who prophesy are in control of their spirit and can take turns. (1 Corinthians 14:32)

Another point Paul made about order in the Corinthian church meetings had to do with taking turns.

Read 1 Corinthians 14:32 in the margin. According to this verse, why should those who prophesied be able to take turns?

In Paul's letter to the church of Galatia, we find that self-control is included in the fruit of the Spirit (see Galatians 5:23). When the Holy Spirit is in control of our lives, we have control over our minds and our bodies. When we claim we cannot control our mouths or actions, we are admitting that the Spirit is not in control. The Holy Spirit always reflects God's nature, bringing order rather than chaos.

We should invite the Holy Spirit into every aspect of our lives, including our church services. The presence of chaos should cause us to ask, "Where is the God of order in this?" and "What is the most loving thing to do in this situation?"

Read 1 Corinthians 14:39-40. How did Paul summarize his instructions related to the worship service?

When we claim we cannot control our mouths or actions, we are admitting that the Spirit is not in control. The Holy Spirit always reflects God's nature, bringing order rather than chaos.

Paul called the church to do things properly and in order. As you consider your own life, is God bringing to mind anything that is out of order? If so, how is it causing you a lack of peace?

Paul often began and ended his letters to the churches by praying that the God of peace would be with them. So as we conclude our study today, I pray that the Lord would direct you to solution-oriented steps to help you find peace in your life. Proverbs 19:21 says, "You can make many plans, / but the LORD's purpose will prevail." While you may not understand all that God is doing, trust that His purpose is for good. God isn't flying by the seat of His pants as we often do. We can be thankful that He is a God of order and peace whose ways and thoughts are higher than ours!

Talk with God

Ask God to reveal His purposes for you, and listen for any steps He calls you to take.

WEEKLY WRAP-UP

Note: This wrap-up exercise should take you approximately 6-7 minutes for reading the chapters and a few additional minutes for recording reflections.

Take a few minutes to read 1 Corinthians 12–14 again—either out loud if possible or silently if you are in a public setting. What new insights or applications did the Holy Spirit lift off the page as you read?

Here are some of the highlights from our study this week:

- The Holy Spirit has given each believer a spiritual gift to be used to help one another.
- As part of the body of Christ, we should focus on doing what God has called us to do rather than comparing ourselves with others.
- Some parts of the body that seem the weakest are actually the most necessary.
- Love is the greatest! Without love, our best efforts are futile.
- Love is patient and kind. It is not jealous or boastful or proud or rude. It doesn't demand its own way, is not irritable, and keeps no record of wrongs. It rejoices in the truth and never gives up or loses faith. It is always hopeful and endures through every circumstance. (Amen and Amen!)
- Our view of life is partial and incomplete, so we should err on the side of love and humility.
- We should beware of elevating one gift over another and giving more weight to showy gifts that give us attention.
- Sound teaching should never be neglected at the expense of emotional experience.
- God is a God of order and calls us to peace rather than chaos.

How do these truths—especially the truth that our view of life is partial and incomplete—encourage and challenge you to show love to others?

Digging Deeper

Did you notice that sandwiched into these verses about order in the Corinthian church meetings are two verses about women being silent in church? Did these verses raise questions or concerns for you? If so, you're not alone! Check out one of two online Digging Deeper articles for Week 5, "The Sound of Silence," to gain some cultural context and learn three views surrounding these verses (see AbingdonPress.com /FirstCorinthians).

This week we've seen how Paul helped the Corinthians discover what living love looks like in God's economy. After studying chapter 13, we can agree that we need supernatural help to love people God's way. Only by His Spirit can we truly love those with whom we disagree and heal fractures in the body of Christ. As you reflect on our week of study, I pray you will consider any controversial positions and opinions you hold in your Christian faith. Although we are not to compromise our beliefs, we must be loving in our interactions, remembering that our view is incomplete. The great news is that God's view is absolutely complete. He sits outside of time and holds all things together. As we walk closely with Him, we experience His peace and learn to treasure people as He does.

LIVING LOVE

God calls us to _____ and _____ _____.

- We are to love God and neighbor. (Matthew 22:37-40)

- The love chapter—what God says our love should look like. (1 Corinthians 13:4-7)

- God's love is wide, long, high, and deep and makes us complete. (Ephesians 3:16-19)

One of the ways we love God is to love His _____.

- God wants us to reach out and love. (Matthew 25:34-40)

- If we love God, we must also love our fellow believers. (1 John 4:20-21)

Love is not the absence of _____.

Now we see things imperfectly, like puzzling reflections in a mirror, but then we will see everything with perfect clarity. All that I know now is _____ and _____, but then I will know everything completely, just as God now knows me completely.

(1 Corinthians 13:12)

With this partial and incomplete view, God is asking us to love _____ _____.

Week 6

REAL LIFE

1 Corinthians 15–16

Memory Verses

⁵⁷ But thank God! He gives us victory over sin and death through our Lord Jesus Christ. ⁵⁸ So, my dear brothers and sisters, be strong and immovable. Always work enthusiastically for the Lord, for you know that nothing you do for the Lord is ever useless.

(1 Corinthians 15:57-58)

DAY 1: THE MAIN THING

A few years ago I had the opportunity to spend time with a dear friend and brother in Christ who was battling brain cancer and knew he was in the final weeks of his life. It was my privilege to listen to stories of his family, work, marriage, divorce, parenting, and battle with cancer and write his memoir. His words of faith in all things inspired me to believe and follow God through all the ups and downs of life. My friend wanted the final chapter of the book to contain the gospel truths that had transformed his life in every way.

This week we come to the final chapters of Paul's letter to Corinth. Just as my friend went from telling stories to explaining gospel truths, Paul switched gears from answering questions and sorting out relational conflicts to explaining an important doctrine of faith. He wanted the church at Corinth to gain clarity that their physical bodies would be resurrected, just as Christ was raised from the dead. One commentator points out, "It is no accident that [Paul's] teachings on the cross (1:18–2:16) and resurrection (15:1-58) stand like bookends—or sentinels—at beginning and end of the body of his letter to the Corinthians."[2]

Paul knew the Resurrection is pivotal to the Christian faith. First Corinthians 15 contains more teaching on resurrection than any other chapter in Scripture. I believe that in this letter about unity, gray areas, and controversial subjects, Paul wanted to be sure the believers found common ground on a doctrine of utmost importance.

In order to understand the context of Paul's teaching, we will revisit the circumstances of the original audience. Imagine you are a believer in one of the house churches in Corinth. You have not grown up in a Christian home, because no one at this time has. Every church member's testimony is recent, whether he or she converted from Judaism or pagan idol worship. Here are a few things to keep in mind:

- Corinth was a Greek city, and Greeks did not believe in the resurrection of the dead. This is why some who listened to Paul's preaching in nearby Athens laughed at him when he taught about the Resurrection (see Acts 17:32).

Extra Insight

Scottish commentator William Barclay called 1 Corinthians 15 "one of the greatest and one of the most difficult chapters in the New Testament."[1]

- Some of the Corinthians might have spiritualized the idea of resurrection (as later Gnostics did), believing it to be only of the soul and not of the body.[3]
- A sect or group of Jews called the Sadducees did not believe in life after death (see Acts 23:8). Some Christians in Corinth might have been Sadducees before believing in Jesus.
- The Old Testament concept of afterlife was very limited. For example, Psalm 6:5 says, "For the dead do not remember you. / Who can praise you from the grave?" (See also Psalms 30:9; 88:10-12; 115:17; and Isaiah 38:18.)
- Like many cultures, the Greeks feared death and discussed their ideas about what happened to people after they die. "For the Greeks, immortality lay precisely in getting rid of the body. For them, the resurrection of the body was unthinkable."[4]

As we understand the cultural backdrop, we gain greater insight into Paul's emphasis on bodily resurrection. Paul wanted the church to shed the worldly influence of Greek philosophy, as well as any former religious traditions that denied the concept of a bodily resurrection, and embrace what Christ had taught.

Jesus told her, "I am the resurrection and the life. Anyone who believes in me will live, even after dying." (John 11:25)

Read John 11:25 in the margin. What did Christ say about Himself?

Although the Old Testament's picture of life after death was limited, Jesus provided a fuller revelation that assures us this world is not all there is. Paul expounded upon this assurance, emphasizing the importance of hope for the next life.

Turn to 1 Corinthians 15 and put a placeholder there. What do you learn about the gospel from verses 1 and 2?

Extra Insight

First Corinthians 15 has been called the early church's statement of faith.

Paul began his argument for resurrection with the Corinthians' own experience of life transformation. He reminded them that the gospel is:

- Welcomed or received by believers in Christ. Salvation is not earned; it is a gift that is received.
- Something in which we stand. Salvation provides stability in an unstable world, keeping us from falling.
- The source of our salvation. The verb Paul used is present tense— we have been saved from the penalty of sin and are being saved from the power of sin through our faith in Christ.

Paul reminded the Corinthian believers to hold tenaciously to the truths they knew and had experienced. Like those early believers, we too can be forgetful or "leaky" when it comes to gospel truth. Reflecting on the transforming work the Lord has done in our lives strengthens our faith and helps us hold tightly to truth through the storms of life.

Reflect on the aspects of the gospel that Paul asked the Corinthians to recall by answering the following questions:

What is one of your earliest memories of believing in Jesus? If it seems you always have believed, share one of your earliest memories of hearing about, or praying to Jesus.

How has your faith in Christ brought stability in your life?

How is salvation not only a past experience but also a present reality? What is an example from your life that shows how you are currently being saved through God's power?

After reminding the Corinthian believers to hold on to truth learned from personal experience, Paul talked about others who gave outside credibility to the Resurrection.

According to 1 Corinthians 15:3-4, what source attested to the fact that Christ died, was buried, and then was raised?

Because the New Testament was not complete at the time Paul wrote his letter, most commentators agree that the phrase "according to the Scriptures" refers to the prophecies of the Old Testament and possibly the Gospel writings.

Look up the following passages and write a statement for each to summarize how it refers to Christ's death, burial, and resurrection:

Psalm 16:8-11

Isaiah 53:3-10

Matthew 12:38-41

In making his case for the Resurrection, Paul not only talked about transformative experiences but also referenced the authority of Scripture. We too must look to the Bible when defining essentials of our faith. In order to differentiate between preferences and absolutes, we must go to the Scriptures.

The Bereans provide a good example for us. Acts 17:11 says, "The people of Berea were more open-minded than those in Thessalonica, and they listened eagerly to Paul's message. They searched the Scriptures day after day to see if Paul and Silas were teaching the truth." Like the Bereans, we can approach Scripture with an open mind and teachable spirit, taking into account the cultural context of the original audience and expecting God's Spirit to guide our understanding.

Though Paul did not refer to specific Scriptures in support of Christ's death, burial, and resurrection, he reminded the Corinthians that his teaching on the Resurrection aligned with God's Word.

How has God used His Word in your life recently to confirm truth or direct your thinking?

After citing the Corinthian believers' personal experience of the gospel and the support of Scripture, Paul then discussed the testimony of witnesses to the resurrection of Christ.

Read 1 Corinthians 15:5-11 and list below the people or groups that saw Jesus after His resurrection:

Of all these people, who stands out to you and why?

We can approach Scripture with an open mind and teachable spirit, taking into account the cultural context of the original audience and expecting God's Spirit to guide our understanding.

Cephas, or Peter, stands out to me personally. Peter had denied Christ three times before His death on the cross. So when Jesus appeared to Peter after rising from the grave, it would have been a powerful moment.

Only in Paul's first letter to the Corinthians do we learn that Jesus appeared to five hundred people. Some of the believers in Corinth might have been among those five hundred—or they might have known some of those eyewitnesses.

Verse 7 tells us that Jesus appeared to James, whom many scholars believe was the half-brother of Jesus. What do we learn about Jesus' brothers from John 7:5 (in the margin)?

For even his brothers didn't believe in him. (John 7:5)

After Jesus appeared to many and then ascended to heaven, Scripture reveals a change in His brothers. Acts 1:14 tells us that they were among those who were gathering together for prayer. According to early church history, although James had not believed initially that Jesus was the Messiah, he later became the leader of the church in Jerusalem.[5] It is only in 1 Corinthians 15:7 that we discover James had an encounter with the resurrected Messiah.

Lastly, Paul talked about his own private vision of Jesus (1 Corinthians 15:8). Acts 9:1-31 gives a detailed account of Paul hearing Christ's voice in a blinding encounter on the road to Damascus.

How do you think Paul's reminders of the many eyewitness accounts of the resurrected Christ were encouraging to the believers in Corinth?

The stories in the New Testament of those who saw the resurrected Christ give validity and strength to our own faith. Jesus Himself always wanted to help people grow in faith and believe His message. He never shamed those who doubted.

Read John 20:24-29. Who doubted the resurrection of Jesus?

What proof did he want before he would accept the truth of the Resurrection?

How did Christ respond?

I love that Jesus didn't chastise Thomas for his doubts but helped him believe. He helps us believe, too.

What doubts do you need to bring to Jesus today?

Jesus wants us to come to Him with our doubts and struggles. Doubting reveals a natural process of working through belief.

Jesus wants us to come to Him with our doubts and struggles. Doubting reveals a natural process of working through belief. Study, prayer, and discussion lead us to deeper faith as we work through our doubts. If we suppress our real thoughts and questions, we cannot grow. So when we experience dry times, conflict, or uncertainty about essentials and liberties, let us cling to God's past and present transforming work in our lives, the truth of God's Word (which is alive and active), and the testimony of others who have experienced God at work in their lives.

We serve a living God. Death could not hold Him. He is risen! He is risen, indeed!

Talk with God

Spend some time thanking God for what He has done in your life, praising Him for His Word, bringing Him your doubts and fears, and asking Him to help you grow in faith. If you seek Him, you will find Him!

DAY 2: YOLO

YOLO. By the time I heard this phrase, my children told me it wasn't "in" anymore. It stands for "You Only Live Once." A few years ago it was a cool saying that teens used. They would write it after a hashtag at the end of their texts—#YOLO—as a way to say, "Take risks, do what you want to do, live it up because you only have one life."

The problem with this saying isn't that it's not cool anymore (at least according to the teens under my roof). The problem is that it isn't true! After death we *will* live again—eternally with God in heaven through our acceptance of Christ's sacrifice on the cross as the payment for our sin, or eternally separated from God. In our reading of the next section of 1 Corinthians 15, we'll find Paul addressing a theological misunderstanding regarding the Resurrection that had implications for the way the Corinthian believers lived. We must remember that our doctrine informs our decisions.

We must remember that our doctrine informs our decisions.

Though we may struggle to find specific application for every verse we read today, our study will give us a bigger view of God. So don't worry if the lesson doesn't give you specific action steps for your life. Having a fuller understanding of Jesus and His resurrection has great value.

We saw yesterday that in the first part of chapter 15, Paul reminded the believers of the evidence for Christ's resurrection. Apparently the Corinthian Christians had already accepted this doctrine since, according to verse 1, Paul was repeating what he had preached to them before. Where the Corinthians lacked clarity was in the understanding that Christ's resurrection was a forerunner to a bodily resurrection for all believers. The Greek believers in Corinth could accept that Jesus rose from the dead, but they had trouble making the leap to the idea that they too would be resurrected in body and spirit.

Turn to 1 Corinthians 15 and put a placeholder there. Read verses 12-19, and fill in the blanks below (wording will vary according to the translation, but the concepts will be the same):

If there is no resurrection of the dead, then

Christdas _____ **(vv. 13, 17)**

our preaching is _____ **(v. 14)**

your faith is _____ **(vv. 14, 17)**

the apostles _____ **(v. 15)**

you are _____ **(v. 17)**

all who have died believing in Christ are _____ **(v. 18)**

Now write verse 19 below:

If someone asked you why the Resurrection is vital to the Christian faith, how would you answer?

How does hope in Christ for the next life give you encouragement in your daily struggles in this life?

Paul lived through all sorts of persecution. In his second letter to the Corinthians he talked about the trials he endured:

> 24 *Five different times the Jewish leaders gave me thirty-nine lashes. Three times I was beaten with rods. Once I was stoned.* 25 *Three times I was shipwrecked. Once I spent a whole night and a day adrift at sea.* 26 *I have traveled on many long journeys. I have faced danger from rivers and from robbers. I have faced danger from my own people, the Jews, as well as from the Gentiles. I have faced danger in the cities, in the deserts, and on the seas. And I have faced danger from men who claim to be believers but are not.* 27 *I have worked hard and long, enduring many sleepless nights. I have been hungry and thirsty and have often gone without food. I have shivered in the cold, without enough clothing to keep me warm.*
>
> (2 Corinthians 11:24-27)

Paul said that for Him, living was Christ but dying was even better (Philippians 1:21). After reading all that he endured, I can see why he thought dying would be better!

What are some trials that have caused you to look forward to heaven?

Life is hard. Christ brings purpose, peace, and adventure in the midst of our struggles, but sometimes the only thing that helps us hold on to hope is thinking of the next life. We should remind one another that one day we will no longer live in a cursed world where sickness, conflict, and death bring pain and grief. A passage that brings me comfort and encouragement when life gets me down is found in Paul's letter to the Romans.

Read Romans 8:18-25, and write below two things that believers have to look forward to after death:

1.

2.

One day there will be no more death! When people we love suffer and are taken from us, we grieve—but not as those who have no hope. Thinking about the next life brings us hope to endure this life. We realize our trials are temporary. We remember that God will reveal glory that will make every sacrifice and difficulty worth it.

These verses from Romans liken this life to labor before a child is born. I've gone through labor three times. When I think of my children, labor seems like a distant and faint memory. As painful as those experiences of labor were, they were momentary and brief in light of the amazing gifts of children they produced. This life is like labor—difficult and painful but producing great results.

How do these verses from Romans encourage you in the midst of whatever difficulties you are facing?

Paul talks more about the Resurrection in the following section of chapter 15.

Read 1 Corinthians 15:20-29 and answer the following questions:

What Old Testament reference did Paul make in verses 20 and 23 to explain Christ's resurrection? (See Leviticus 23:10-11 if you aren't sure.)

What person did Paul reference in verses 21-22 in relation to Christ?

Paul made it clear that Christ had been raised, and he used a couple of Old Testament references to help the Corinthians understand the connection between Christ's resurrection and the resurrection of all believers. First, he called Christ the first fruits or first harvest. Under the Jewish sacrificial system, the people gave an offering of the first fruits of the harvest. In fact, barley could not be sold in the markets until a special offering of first fruits was given to the Lord. One scholar explains the comparison for us: "Just as new barley could not be used until the first fruits had been duly offered, so the new harvest of life could not come until Jesus had been raised from the dead."[7]

Jesus' resurrection was like the offering of first fruits. It was a beginning rather than an end in itself.

Paul then explained that death came through Adam but life comes through Christ. He reminded the Corinthians why they needed a redeemer and a resurrection, and he went on to say that in the end Christ will defeat every enemy—every ruler, power, authority, and eventually death (vv. 24-26). We do not have to fear because we know that Christ has won the victory through the cross and ultimately will destroy every enemy!

> **We do not have to fear because we know that Christ has won the victory through the cross and ultimately will destroy every enemy!**

Next, Paul helped the Corinthians apply these truths in their lives.

Read 1 Corinthians 15:30-34. How does this passage address YOLO thinking?

The surrounding culture had bought into the mind-set of "feast and drink, for tomorrow we die" (v. 32). Classical literature and modern movies are full of this kind of thinking. Those rulers, powers, and authorities that Christ ultimately will destroy propagate this worldview. God calls us to stamp eternity in our eyes while the enemy tempts us to live only for today.

How is the message of YOLO (instant gratification) promoted in our culture?

Reread 1 Corinthians 15:33-34. What practical instruction did Paul give to keep his readers from falling into YOLO thinking?

We forget that every decision is a spiritual decision. How we spend our time, treasures, and talents echoes into eternity.

"Bad company corrupts good character" (1 Corinthians 15:33). This is a verse we often teach our children, encouraging them to choose their friends carefully. Paul was warning the church in Corinth to be careful about who they hung around. When we spend the majority of our time with people who are focusing on the short game rather than keeping eternity in mind, we can be corrupted by their thinking. We forget that every decision is a spiritual decision. How we spend our time, treasures, and talents echoes into eternity.

When I drift away from an eternal perspective, I get caught up thinking about my house, clothes, and outward appearance; and I tend to look for my identity in what I do or who I know rather than in Christ alone. Recently I was cleaning my house and feeling discontent because of the repairs that are needed and the upgrades I would like to make. Sometimes I watch too many home improvement television shows, which breed discontent in my heart. When I get into a YOLO mentality, I forget that all these things will burn up on Judgment Day; only what I've done for Christ will last.

Don't get me wrong. God created beauty and gave us the desire to make things beautiful. Repairing or decorating our homes is not inherently sinful. However, when I become overly fixated on temporal things to the point of discontent and ingratitude, I need to shift my focus to what will matter in eternity.

When have you been so consumed with the things of this life that you forgot about what will matter in the next?

Think of a few people who help you keep an eternal perspective, and write their names below. How can you pursue time with one or more of these individuals this week?

Sometimes the world's mind-set influences our thinking more than we realize. Though we are called to be salt and light in the world, we need the Holy Spirit to illuminate when we are allowing the world to influence us negatively. Spending time with Christian friends who help us to keep our focus on eternity can help us to stay balanced.

Throughout his letter Paul has called for liberty in gray areas, but now he calls the church to stand without compromise on an essential point of theology: the Resurrection. According to God's Word, the Resurrection is a nonnegotiable—an absolute of the faith that unites us as believers in Christ. God calls us to revisit this basic tenet of our faith, remembering that there is more to this life than what we can touch, taste, and feel. God has placed eternity in our hearts (Ecclesiastes 3:11).

In his book *Rumors of Another World*, Phil Yancey writes about the contrast of what we see online and in magazines in the grocery aisle and what people truly value at the end of this life. He writes:

> Net worth, body shape, muscle tone, beauty secrets, possessions: each of these is transitory. I have attended my share of funerals, and not once have friends and family members eulogized about the deceased's bank account or physical shape or surround-sound stereo system. Instead, they speak of qualities like kindness and generosity and love for family.[9]

The more we talk about the Resurrection, the more we are able to live love in the midst of our disagreements. The truth of eternal life helps us realign our heads and hearts with the habit of treasuring people rather than transitory things. As you approach the ups and downs of the week ahead, I pray that the promise of a future resurrection will encourage you to wholeheartedly pursue love and kindness even in the midst of earthly concerns.

Talk with God

Give God praise that although death came through Adam, Jesus came to bring us life! Ask God to show you how temporal thinking is keeping

> The truth of eternal life helps us realign our heads and hearts with the habit of treasuring people rather than transitory things.

you from living in light of eternity. Invite the Lord to stamp eternity in your eyes so that you can love God and people rather than material things that will fade away.

DAY 3: NOTHING WASTED

One day my friend and I were joking about whether she still eats oatmeal for lunch every day. I used to tease her regularly about her obsessive eating habits and lack of variety. She laughed and said that lately she doesn't even make herself a lunch. After making grilled cheese or peanut butter sandwiches for her preschooler and toddler, she usually just eats whatever they leave on their plates. Her boys are going through a picky eating phase, and she hates to see food wasted.

I can identify with not being a fan of waste. My grandmother often told me stories of living through the Depression. When I steamed the nice white paper from some of the gifts at my wedding shower so that I could reuse it to wrap my bridesmaids' gifts, my parents laughed and said that I take after my grandma.

God isn't into waste either. Nothing we do for Him is useless. Even when something doesn't work out right and it seems we've wasted our time, money, or talents, God uses our efforts in ways we cannot begin to understand in this life. The Resurrection reminds us that in God's economy, nothing we do for Him is futile.

Paul wanted the Corinthians to gain a fuller understanding of the Resurrection and to be encouraged that many things that seem useless in this life have value in the next. His teaching on resurrection shapes our own understanding as well and motivates us toward godly living.

I love it when Scripture includes object lessons, using things we understand in the physical realm to help us understand parallel spiritual truths.

Many things that seem useless in this life have value in the next.

Read 1 Corinthians 15:35-42, and complete the chart below:

Verses	Illustration Paul Used	Insights about the Resurrection
36-38		
39-40		
41-42		

Just as a seed has to be sown in the ground and die in order to be transformed into a plant, so our earthly bodies must die before they are resurrected. When they are raised to new life, our physical bodies will not merely be put back together. Warren Wiersbe puts it this way: *"Resurrection is not reconstruction*. Nowhere does the Bible teach that, at the resurrection, God will 'put together the pieces' and return to us our former bodies."[10] Instead, we will have new bodies that are much better than the "seed" sown in the ground. This knowledge of the Resurrection motivates us to prioritize eternal concerns over earthly ones.

When we bought our current home, I was so excited to plant flowers. That first fall, I buried tulip bulbs around the mailbox and in the front flowerbeds. They weren't much to look at when I covered them with soil, but by the following spring those ugly bulbs had transformed into gorgeous, colorful tulips. Like a tulip bulb, our end game is not a buried, unattractive lump. One day we will experience new life as we spring into our spiritual bodies.

After Jesus rose from the grave, He appeared to His followers. His resurrected body gives us some clues about what our new bodies might be like. Jesus walked through walls and disappeared from one location only to reappear in another, but He also ate food and allowed the disciples to touch him (see Luke 24:33-43; John 20:19-20). I don't know about you, but the idea that my spiritual body might be something like that gets me excited!

Read 1 John 3:2 in the margin. What two things do we have to look forward to when Christ appears?

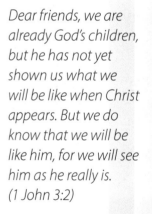

Dear friends, we are already God's children, but he has not yet shown us what we will be like when Christ appears. But we do know that we will be like him, for we will see him as he really is. (1 John 3:2)

We will be like the resurrected Jesus! Perhaps we will be able to walk through walls and move quickly while still being able to recognize each other and enjoy food. While Scripture only gives us a glimpse of the exciting possibilities, this glimpse helps us endure the realities of our "tulip bulb" lives. For me, these realities include housework, backaches, piles of work, and difficult people.

What are the realities of your "tulip bulb" life?

What is one thing about having a resurrected body that you are looking forward to?

Paul encouraged the Corinthian believers by mentioning a few benefits that spiritual bodies have over earthly ones.

Read 1 Corinthians 15:43-44, and complete the chart below:

Earthly bodies are buried:	Heavenly bodies are raised:
v. 43	
v. 43	
v. 44	

God takes our broken and weak natural human bodies and transforms them into glorious, strong spiritual bodies.

Now read 1 Corinthians 15:45-57 and answer the following questions:

What kind of bodies cannot inherit the kingdom of God? (v. 50)

What secret does Paul share with the church at Corinth? (v. 51)

What is the sting that results in death? (v. 56)

Why can we give thanks? (v. 57)

One commentator points out that "the literal translation of 1 Corinthians 15:57 is, 'But thanks be to God *who keeps on giving us the victory* through our Lord Jesus Christ.'"[11] Because of Christ's finished work on the cross, sin and death have lost their sting.

When I think of my loved ones who have died and who are now with Christ, I like to envision the new spiritual bodies they will have for all eternity. My dear Uncle Bill died this year, leaving behind a wealth of people who loved and admired him. At the memorial service we heard stories from friends, family, and coworkers about the integrity, strong work ethic, and kindness of this incredible man of God. I don't know many other men who exemplify the humility, commitment to God's Word, generosity, and love of my Uncle Bill. Though his dying body barely resembled the man I remembered, I like to imagine his perfect spiritual body, which will be even better than the healthy body of his youth.

Take a moment to reflect on loved ones you have lost who now are with Christ. Envision them at peace in Christ's presence. Now envision them with the new spiritual bodies they will receive. Write a short prayer below thanking God that death is truly swallowed up in victory through Christ:

Now we come to the final verse of 1 Corinthians 15. It's our memory verse for the week and one of my favorite verses in all of Scripture.

Read 1 Corinthians 15:58. According to this verse, what does Paul say we are to be and do—and why?

Be: _____

Do: _____

Because: _____

In light of all the resurrection truths we've learned in chapter 15, we must respond. Truth helps us realign our thinking and living. Just as our physical bodies will be transformed, so our earthly living can be transformed with purpose. Because there is more to this life than what we can see, we live in anticipation.

We do not have to live weak and unstable lives; instead we are to take a posture that is strong and immovable. Even when we are tired and discouraged, we are to work enthusiastically. Everything we do matters! Nothing we do for the Lord is useless.

> **Because there is more to this life than what we can see, we live in anticipation.**

Nothing includes everything from laundry (serving) to ministry (investing) to careers (providing). We can work enthusiastically on both the smallest and the biggest of tasks. God doesn't waste anything. Not a crumb of prayer, service, study, or manual labor will be swept away.

What have you been doing lately that seems to be a waste of your time, talents, or treasures?

Be encouraged that if you are doing it for the Lord, He will use it for His glory!

Some time ago I had a book signing that was very poorly attended and seemed to be a waste of time. I remember asking God if I had not heard Him correctly about it. Several weeks later, I got a call from someone who extended a great opportunity for me to teach and serve in just the capacity I feel called. At the end of the long conversation, I asked the person, "How did you get my name and number?" The individual told me that someone I had talked with at the small book signing had recommended me for this larger opportunity. What I had seen as a waste ended up opening a much bigger door. God was reminding me yet again not to manipulate but to listen to Him and then obey.

What seems like a waste to us might reap big results later. God's Holy Spirit knows much better than we do where we should go and what we should do. Our responsibility is to seek Him and follow where He leads. When we do, we can live in His strength and work enthusiastically for Him, remembering that He doesn't waste a thing. My grandma would say "Amen" to that!

Talk with God

Quiet your heart and mind and spend some time listening to God. Ask Him to speak His words of life, transformation, and purpose over you. Write in the margin any specific insights or truths from today's study that God wants you to embrace.

DAY 4: LIVING AND GIVING WITH LOVE

In his letter to the Corinthians, Paul mastered the art of switching gears. After writing in depth about resurrection theology, Paul became extremely practical. One moment Paul was describing spiritual bodies and the next he wrote, "Now about that offering" (see 1 Corinthians 16:1).

While most commentators mention this sudden change from doctrinal to practical, some have suggested that discussing the offering on the heels of resurrection shows the integral nature of faith and works.

When it comes to talking about money, we Christians have a tendency to fall into two extremes. One of my friends comes from a church background where guilt and pressure often were applied to the offering. Church leaders would count the offering, and if it wasn't enough, they would take up another one with a lot of "encouragement." Other churches ignore the subject of money, never teaching on a topic that Jesus emphasized in his ministry. In addition to telling many parables that involved money, Jesus said, "Freely you have received; freely give" (Matthew 10:8b NIV).

Early in our marriage, I explained to Sean that in order to pay our rent on the first of the month, we would need to withhold that week's planned giving to our church. He wanted to write a check to the church anyway. We lived in Canada, and I did not yet have a work permit; so I had lots of time to fret over finances. Sean wanted to trust God while I told him we needed to be practical. I can be pretty persistent when I want my way, so we decided not to give that Sunday with the intention of doubling up the next week. Late that night Sean remembered that someone at church had given him an envelope, which he had put in his coat pocket. He opened it and read a note written by a sweet widow in our church, who explained that the Lord had laid on her heart the desire to pay our rent that month. Enclosed were five one-hundred dollar bills. God was faithful even when I wasn't!

I have reflected often on that experience. Since that time Sean has had his way when it comes to writing the check on Sunday, and God has continued to be faithful in our lives.

Although the New Testament doesn't give us exact figures or percentages for our giving, it teaches us that in light of eternity we should invest our resources wisely in Kingdom work. In chapter 16 of Paul's letter, we find two general principles for giving. Let's look at each one and see how the Lord would have us apply it in our lives.

1. Give Generously

Giving to those in need provides a way to unite followers of Christ. We may disagree about how we give and how the money is used, but we can find common ground in reaching out to those with genuine physical needs. The collection Paul refers to in chapter 16 is for the church in Jerusalem, which had experienced famine and persecution. Here we find some guiding principles that we can apply today.

Extra Insight

"Jesus told twenty-nine parables in the Gospels, and sixteen of them have to do with people and their money."[12]

Read 1 Corinthians 16:1-4. Then refer to verse 2 to answer the following questions:

Who should participate in the offering?

How often should they put money aside?

In what amounts should each person give?

From this one verse we find that giving applies to all believers. Each of us can give something. This verse also teaches us that giving should be regular or systematic. Paul asked the Corinthian believers to give weekly because that was how often they gathered. He also asked that money be set aside ahead of time so that collections would not have to be made on the spot during his visit. Paul was for regular, planned giving rather than emotional or pressured giving. Although weekly giving isn't a rigid standard to be unilaterally applied, contributions should have a consistent pattern.

Another principle from this verse pertains to proportionate giving. Paul did not ask everyone to give the same amount. Some could give more and others less depending on their income. We see proportionate giving in the Old Testament as well as in the Jews' system of tithing. There were two tithes:

1. An annual 10 percent of income for the maintenance of the Levites (see Leviticus 27:30 and Numbers 18:21).
2. A second 10 percent brought to Jerusalem for the Lord's feasts (see Deuteronomy 14:22). Every third year, however, this second tithe was kept at home for the poor (see Deuteronomy 14:28).

Christians are to give regularly, proportionately, and from the heart.

What is different in the New Testament is that no longer is there a specific percentage or requirement of law related to giving. Instead, Christians are to give regularly, proportionately, and from the heart. Rather than hard and fast rules, Christ calls us to give sacrificially. C. S. Lewis said it this way, "I am afraid the only safe rule is to give *more* than we can spare."[13]

One last principle we find in these verses has to do with integrity in administering funds. Paul said he would write letters of recommendation for those who would handle the money. As we well know, money can be used for unity and helping others, but it also provides a temptation for greed or theft. As we consider where we give our personal resources, we should look for integrity in those who administer funds.

Take a moment to consider your own personal giving. Here are some questions to ask yourself:

- Am I investing my personal finances in God's kingdom work?
- Am I practicing regular, planned giving or sporadic giving whenever I feel like it?
- Am I contributing in proportion to my income?
- How do I evaluate the organizations where I make consistent donations?

What changes in your current pattern of giving, if any, might God be calling you to make? Spend a moment in prayer, and then respond below.

2. Take Opportunities

Paul switches gears again in verses 5-9, shifting the topics from the offering to his personal plans. This brings us to a second principle for giving.

Read 1 Corinthians 16:5-9, and list below a few of Paul's intentions or plans:

We all make plans. What we notice here is that Paul laid out short, measurable ideas for the future, staying flexible so that God could correct his course at any time. As another New Testament writer urges us to remember, it is God who directs our steps:

> [13] *Now listen, you who say, "Today or tomorrow we will go to this or that city, spend a year there, carry on business and make money."* [14] *Why, you do not even know what will happen tomorrow. What is your life? You are a mist that appears for a little while and then vanishes.* [15] *Instead, you ought to say, "If it is the Lord's will, we will live and do this or that."*
>
> *(James 4:13-15 NIV)*

Extra Insight

Organizations such as the Evangelical Council for Financial Accountability (ECFA) exist to help believers investigate the organizations where they invest their resources for the Kingdom.

Having just discussed the Resurrection, Paul didn't want the people to sit around waiting for Christ's return. He showed that he was making plans but holding to them loosely. He was using the resources God had given him, but he admitted that God might have something else in mind.

As we consider our own plans, we can learn from Paul to take the opportunities God gives us. We can use three S's to help us:

Spirit: God guides us with the Holy Spirit. Jesus said the Holy Spirit will guide us into all truth (see John 16:13).

Scripture: God guides us with Scripture. Just as Paul studied and relied on Scripture, we can look to God's Word for help in making our plans.

Sense: God guides us with sense or reason. Paul used the sense God had given him, explaining the reasoning for his travel plans (1 Corinthians 16:5-9).

Put an X on the line where you fall on this continuum:

I usually fly by   I always set goals
the seat of my pants   and make plans

What opportunities currently are before you?

What flexible plans might the Lord be calling you to make? (If nothing comes to mind, chew on this question for a few days and listen for God's leading.)

Write the two main principles from today's lesson below:

1.

2.

Put a check mark beside the principle that resonates most strongly with you today.

Even though Paul's letter takes an abrupt turn here in chapter 16, we've discovered that God's truth calls us to action. God asks us to invest in His Kingdom and love others sacrificially by giving our financial resources and our time. While we can never outgive our generous God, giving financially and taking opportunities are two of the many ways we can live love.

Talk with God

Spend some time in prayer, asking God to reveal any ways you need to grow regarding your use of money and opportunities. Remember that both are provided by the Lord. Rather than asking God what you should give, ask what you should keep of all that He has so generously provided in your life.

DAY 5: LOVING PEOPLE

As we come to the close of our study, I love that we are ending on the topic of treasuring people. I pray that if someone asks you what God taught you through this study, the idea of loving people will be at the forefront of your mind.

Jesus invested in people. He taught, ate, walked, and even spent time in boats with people. Paul also mentored and lived life alongside others. Christianity means embracing community. But people sure do make things messy, don't they? We are complicated and emotional beings, and we struggle with sin. One of my pastor friends jokes that he loves the church but it's the people that drive him crazy. Yet the church *is* the people. Jesus established His church not as a building or a worship service but as a group of people—imperfect people with imperfect leaders.

I've listened to so many individuals tell stories of church heartbreak. Leaders have made bad decisions. Members have felt left out. People have misunderstood one another's motives. While we must acknowledge our pain, we cannot expect too much of broken people. People will let us down. But God never will!

We've seen that Paul expressed his disappointment to the church in Corinth throughout this letter. He addressed sexual sin, legal disputes, favoritism, and inappropriate forms of worship. Yet he wasn't ready to give up on the church he had planted. Instead, he wanted to visit them, help them, and love them.

With so many churches in our communities today, it's easy to give up on one another when things get complicated. We can move on to the next church for a few years until things go wrong there. While legitimate reasons exist for leaving a church, sometimes we give up too soon. Even when the Holy Spirit moves us to a new community of believers, we still are called to love the people we've left behind. We are holy co-laborers in God's kingdom.

> God asks us to invest in His Kingdom and love others sacrificially by giving our financial resources and our time.

Extra Insight

In his final greeting (1 Corinthians 16:22), Paul switched from Greek to Aramaic with the word *Maranatha.*
—"Our Lord Comes."[14]

As we finish Paul's letter today, let's apply some practical truths about relationships to help us love one another well—even when we disagree.

Read 1 Corinthians 16:10-20, and list some of the people Paul mentioned:

Paul mentioned various people in his life, who represent different kinds of relationships:

- Timothy, someone he mentored (mentoring relationships)
- Apollos, a person with whom he disagreed (relationships with other believers)
- Stephanus, Fortunatus, and Achaicus, Greek church leaders (relationships with church leaders)
- Aquila and Priscilla, close ministry partners and friends (nourishing relationships)

Let's look at these relationships and consider our own relationships as well.

Mentoring Relationships

Paul asked the church to receive young Timothy. Paul knew the tensions and disagreements among the church at Corinth would be a lot for a young pastor like Timothy to handle, so he appealed to the church not to treat him with contempt. Timothy was Paul's representative, and some of the harsh admonitions in Paul's letter might have left members with a bias against Timothy. Through his relationship with Timothy, Paul invested in the next generation. He was a giver and Timothy was a receiver.

Though all relationships have some give and take, God calls us to have some relationships in our lives where we are more of a giver or mentor. Sometimes a mentoring relationship is draining. Other times it brings us great joy as we see growth in our mentee.

When God called our family to plant a church, a wonderful woman who is about twenty years farther down the path of being a church planter's wife agreed to mentor me. We set planned meetings, celebrated wins, and worked through challenges. I made action plans, and she prayed for me and held me accountable. This is a fairly one-sided relationship. She has others who invest in her, but she is clearly the giver in our relationship.

Who is a mentor in your faith journey?

Who are the people in your life God has called you to invest in?

What is a practical way you can invest in one of these people this week?

Relationships with Other Believers

Paul also mentioned Apollos, one of the leaders mentioned in chapter 1 who was favored by some of the Corinthians. Here in chapter 16 we learn that Paul had encouraged Apollos to visit Corinth in spite of the Apollos fan club there (v. 12). Paul wasn't territorial about people. We also discover that although he gave instructions and advice to his peer, he left it to him to hear from God personally. Paul wanted Apollos to go to Corinth, but Apollos wasn't willing at the time. They disagreed! These two believers had a regular, messy relationship. Yet despite their disagreement, Paul acknowledged the value and importance of Apollos's ministry.

How do you respond to other believers when you see a subject differently than they do, especially if it has to do with people you love? Do you have a tendency to compete and compare, or do you choose to collaborate?

When we remember that almost everything except people is temporal, we begin to value our sisters and brothers in Christ more. Jesus has declared us holy through His shed blood, and we should treat one another as such. Though we may disagree on many issues, we will live together in eternity.

We don't have to align in every area to love and value one another. God valued us enough to send His Son to die for us, so we should collaborate with others rather than compete and compare.

Is there another believer you have a disagreement with right now? If so, write below a tangible way you can show love to this person in the midst of your disagreement. (Remember that love and approval are not the same thing!)

> Jesus has declared us holy through His shed blood, and we should treat one another as such.

People matter. They are eternal. God calls us to see them the way He does—through the lens of love!

Relationships with Church Leaders

Next Paul mentioned Stephanas and his household—some of the first believers in Greece—as well as Fortunatus and Achaicus. Paul expressed gratitude for their hard work and asked the church in Corinth to appreciate them and all those who were serving well. This was a call to support those who lead in the church.

It isn't easy to be in charge. So many things take place behind the scenes. Many opinions are expressed. A good leader must consider everyone, spend time in God's presence, and study God's Word to determine the best course of action for the church. Paul reminds us that although they don't always get it right, our imperfect leaders deserve our appreciation.

List a few servant leaders in your church, whether they rock babies in the nursery, teach God's Word, or help with the youth group. Ask the Lord to show you a practical way you can express appreciation to each person this week, writing the idea beside his or her name:

Nourishing Relationships

The last people Paul mentioned were Aquila and Priscilla, who were ministry partners and friends of Paul's. Here are some quick facts about Paul's relationship with Aquila and Priscilla:

- They were of Jewish descent, so they shared a common religious background with Paul. (Acts 18:2)
- They were tentmakers by trade, as was Paul. (Acts 18:3)
- Their names appear six times in the New Testament as leaders in the church. (Acts 18:2; Acts 18:18; Acts 18:26; Romans 16:3; 1 Corinthians 16:19; 2 Timothy 4:19)
- Priscilla and Aquila helped Paul plant the church at Corinth but packed up and left with him when he went to Ephesus. (Acts 18:18)
- Priscilla and Aquila hosted a church in their home (1 Corinthians 16:19)
- Priscilla and Aquila helped explain the gospel to others (Acts 18:26)

- Paul had a special relationship with Aquila and Priscilla. They traveled together, worked alongside each other, and led the church together. Theirs was a nourishing relationship.

We all need relationships with other Christians that are mutually nourishing. Time spent together leaves both parties feeling stronger and encouraged. That does not mean we will never disagree or have to work through problems, but generally we look forward to our time together. These are people of faith that we want to be like. I've heard it said, "If you want to know what you are like, look around at your closest friends." We all need like-minded friends we can serve Jesus alongside.

Who are the people of faith with whom you find a lot of common ground?

If you aren't sure you have any kindred relationships similar to what Paul experienced with Aquila and Priscilla, I would encourage you to pursue some.

When Sean and I first moved to Ohio, we kept inviting couples over for dinner. Some of those nights were draining; others were neutral. But in the process we found some close, nourishing friends that we did life with for many years.

Of course, we must be flexible and nonexclusive even in these nourishing relationships. People move. God calls families in different directions. At times conflict busts up what once was a close relationship. Only Jesus will never let us down. But God gives us the gift of special people to laugh with and love on our spiritual journeys.

Spend a moment reviewing your relationships. Do you have a balance of different kinds of relationships in your life? When I have too many draining relationships at one time, I can feel spiritually empty and in need of refreshment. Other times I surround myself primarily with nourishing people and realize I've neglected other people with genuine needs. Of course, we should not label or categorize people in terms of these relationships. Depending on what is going on in my life, I can be a nourishing friend or a draining friend. So let's not put tags on our relationships. Instead, let's take Paul's advice to love as God leads.

As we close our study, reread 1 Corinthians 16:13-14 and write Paul's five final instructions to the Corinthians:

1.

We don't have to compromise our convictions in order to love. God calls us to stand firm in our faith. But with strength and courage, we can love other people.

2.

3.

4.

5.

Paul calls the church to do *everything* with love. We don't have to compromise our convictions in order to love. God calls us to stand firm in our faith. But with strength and courage, we can love other people. Messy people. Complicated people. Easy-to-love people. All people.

How do these truths resonate in your life and relationships right now?

We come now to the final words of Paul's letter. Read 1 Corinthians 16:21-24, and write verse 24 below:

In keeping with the overarching theme of his letter, Paul ended with love. In no other epistle did he send his love. Typically he ended his letters by praying the grace of God over the church (see Galatians 5:18; Ephesians 6:24; Philippians 4:23; and Colossians 4:18). But to this church that was struggling to get along, Paul added the final words, "My love to all of you in Christ Jesus." Though he had addressed some difficult issues, Paul wanted them to be assured of his great love for them. And he made it clear that his love for them was rooted in Christ Jesus—for it is only through Christ that we are able to love.

Hold on to that powerful truth, my friend, as you seek to live love in the days to come. Jesus gives us His patient, kind, and sacrificial love so that in His power we can love one another—even when we disagree!

Talk with God

Let's end our study by praising God that He is the very definition of love. He certainly doesn't agree with many of our motives, choices, or actions, but He loves us anyway! List in the margin a few characteristics of God's love (refer to 1 Corinthians 13), and spend some time giving Him glory for loving us so faithfully.

WEEKLY WRAP-UP

Note: This wrap-up exercise covers the chapters we've studied this week as well as the main concepts from the entire study. Allow 10-15 minutes for the full exercise.

Take a few minutes to read 1 Corinthians 15–16 again—either out loud if possible or silently if you are in a public setting. What new insights or applications did the Holy Spirit lift off the page as you read?

Now, rather than reviewing the highlights from our study of chapters 15 and 16, let's take a few moments to review the main concepts from all six weeks of our study.

Read the following summary chart, and put a star beside the week that resonates most strongly with you during this season of your life:

Week of Study	Main Themes	Reflection Questions
1. In Christ Alone Chapters 1–2	The letter opened with the gospel and our identity in Christ. Seeing ourselves and one another as holy and loved by God sets the foundation we need for dealing with our disagreements.	Where do you find your identity? It's so easy to seek worth in our careers, possessions, or the eyes of others. Remember that if you have called on the name of Christ, He has made you holy.
2. Growing Up Chapters 3–5	Like a good father, Paul wanted his children in the faith to grow. Their petty disagreements and spiritual pride were keeping them from building with materials that would last forever. Paul admonished them to stop judging one another and merely talking about spiritual things. He reminded them that the kingdom of God is living by God's power.	Is your walk with Christ strong and growing? What does your spiritual diet look like? Are you talking about God but not experiencing the power to change? God wants us to grow continually in faith so that we can invest in others. How might soul junk food be hindering your ability to live by God's power and store up treasure in heaven?

> Jesus gives us His patient, kind, and sacrificial love so that in His power we can love one another—even when we disagree!

3. Everybody's Doing It Chapters 6–8	Sexual sin, idolatry, and lawsuits abounded in Corinthian culture. The church struggled not to be sucked into worldly thinking and excuse behaviors that were unbiblical.	How are you struggling to live in the world but not be of it? What influence does your surrounding culture have in your life? Just because "everybody's doing it" doesn't mean it is beneficial for your spiritual life.
4. Beyond Ourselves Chapters 9–11	Paul called the believers to find common ground with others so that they might share the gospel. He said individual rights are secondary to winning souls for Christ. He encouraged the church to run spiritually just as athletes train physically with discipline and passion.	Where has selfishness isolated you from other believers? Where can you find common ground with others in order to share the gospel? How can you run your spiritual race with greater discipline and purpose?
5. Living Love Chapters 12–14	Love is the greatest. Paul defined the reality of God's love—which stands for truth and treats others respectfully and patiently in the process. He called the Corinthian church to apply the principles of love in their conflict over spiritual gifts.	How are you loving others lately? Does it look like a picture of 1 Corinthians 13? It's harder than it sounds on paper. How does realizing that we see an incomplete picture help you extend love to those with whom you disagree?
6. Real Life Chapters 15–16	These physical bodies won't last forever. They will be resurrected to spiritual bodies. In light of that, Paul reminded the church that nothing they did for the Lord ever would be wasted. He called them to give generously, take opportunities, and invest in people. Everything is to be done with love.	How does your view of the next life bring perspective to your current decisions? What changes is God calling you to make in your giving and time management? Think of relationships God is calling you to invest in, and ask the Lord to help you do everything in love!

How do the themes of the week that you starred echo into your current circumstances?

Now write a few brief responses to the reflection questions listed for that week (right column of the chart):

I don't know about you, but studying Paul's letter to Corinth has caused my brain to hurt at times! Those passages that are especially "wrapped" in culture forced me to my knees. I found myself asking the Lord to help me make sense of verses that seemed contrary to my understanding of Him. Other verses rang so true in my life, exposing areas of weakness I didn't know I had. I especially resonated with the Corinthian believers' struggle not to be sucked into what everyone else around them was doing. Worldly culture so easily seeps in, and often we do not even realize we are choosing what is temporal instead of what is eternal in regards to our time and relationships.

Watching believers belittle one another—whether they are disagreeing on social media forums or in person—breaks my heart. I hope it breaks your heart too. And we know it grieves the Lord! He calls us to live love even when—or perhaps *especially when*—we disagree. My prayer is that we will see other believers as holy and loved by God. Then perhaps as the world watches us love one another, they will want to know our loving God. Let's choose to live love!

VIDEO VIEWER GUIDE: WEEK 6

REAL LIFE

God offers us His _____ power to help us live _____ lives.

- The Spirit of God lives within us. (Romans 8:10-12)

- Sometimes we live like spiritual paupers, yet we have resurrection power within us.

Don't be fooled by those who say such things, "for _____ company corrupts _____ character." Think carefully about what is right, and stop sinning. For to your shame I say that some of you don't know God at all.

(1 Corinthians 15:33-34)

- We pick up the moral accents of those we surround ourselves with.

Our _____ in Christ is so much _____ than this life.

- Everyone who belongs to Christ will be given new life. (1 Corinthians 15:20-22)

- We can damage others trying to pull out the weeds. (Matthew 13:24-30)

- Sometimes God tells us to speak truth in people's lives, but we must do so carefully and sensitively.

Brokenness motivates us to think about the future _____ _____ that we are going to have.

- Our broken bodies will be raised as spiritual bodies. (1 Corinthians 15:43-44)

- Sometimes God allows us to struggle because He is doing something in us; He wants us to fly.

- Death is swallowed up in victory. (1 Corinthians 15:54-57)

Nothing we do for the Lord is ever _____.

God doesn't waste a thing we do for Him. (1 Corinthians 15:58)

Notes

Week 1

1. "About the Moravian Church," http://www.moravian.org/the-moravian-church/about-the-moravian-church/.
2. Craig L. Blomberg, *The NIV Application Commentary: 1 Corinthians* (Grand Rapids: Zondervan, 1994), 19.
3. Gordon Fee, *The New International Commentary on the New Testament: The First Epistle to the Corinthians, Revised Edition* (Grand Rapids: Eerdmans, 1987), 37.
4. Blomberg, 43.
5. Ray C. Stedman, *Letters to a Troubled Church: 1 and 2 Corinthians* (Grand Rapids: Discovery House, 2007), 12.
6. "Nous," http://www.biblestudytools.com/lexicons/greek/kjv/nous.html.
7. "Gnome," http://www.biblestudytools.com/lexicons/greek/kjv/gnome.html.
8. "Sheeple," Urban Dictionary, http://www.urbandictionary.com/define.php?term=Sheeple.
9. Blomberg, 48.
10. Stedman, 20.
11. Blomberg, 44.
12. N. T. Wright, *Paul for Everyone: 1 Corinthians* (Louisville: Westminster John Knox Press, 2004), 15.
13. Stedman, 32.
14. Blomberg, 61.

Week 2

1. C. K. Barrett, *The First Epistle to the Corinthians* (New York and Evanston: Harper & Row, 1968), 80.
2. Timothy Keller with Kathy Keller, *The Meaning of Marriage: Facing the Complexities of Commitment with the Wisdom of God* (New York: Penguin Books, 2011), 48.
3. Frank E. Gaebelein, general editor, *The Expositor's Bible Commentary Volume 10* (Grand Rapids: Zondervan, 1976), 207.
4. Warren Wiersbe, *Be Wise: Discern the Difference between Man's Knowledge and God's Wisdom: NT Commentary: 1 Corinthians* (Colorado Springs: David C. Cook, 1982), 53.
5. John MacArthur, Jr., *The MacArthur New Testament Commentary: 1 Corinthians* (Chicago: Moody Press, 1984), 79.
6. Richard B. Hays, *First Corinthians: Interpretation: A Bible Commentary for Teaching and Preaching* (Louisville: Westminster John Knox, 2011), 51.
7. MacArthur, 79.
8. Gaebelein, 207.
9. Wiersbe, 54.
10. Stedman, 65.
11. Barclay, 43.
12. William Barclay, *The New Daily Study Bible: The Letters to the Corinthians* (Louisville: 13. Westminster John Knox, 2002), 47.
13. Charles R. Erdman, *The First Epistle of Paul to the Corinthians* (Grand Rapids: Baker, 1983), 55.
14. Hays, 66.
15. Ibid., 73.
16. Wright, 62.
17. MacArthur, 123.

18. Weirsbe, 75-76.
19. Ibid., 73.

Week 3

1. Blomberg, 117.
2. Barclay, 59.
3. MacArthur, 136.
4. Wright, 65.
5. Wiersbe, 77.
6. Gaebelein, 221.
7. Hays, 93.
8. Wright, 86.
9. MacArthur, 146.
10. Wright, 75.
11. Wiersbe, 85.
12. Barrett, 154.
13. Erdman, 87.
14. Stedman, 123.
15. Wiersbe, 100.
16. Stedman, 119-120.
17. Gaebelein, 240.
18. Hays, 145.

Week 4

1. Wiersbe, 111.
2. Ibid., 112.
3. Joe Battaglia, *The Politically Incorrect Jesus: Living Boldly in a Culture of Unbelief* (Racine: Broadstreet Publishing, 2014), 43.
4. Barclay, 99.
5. Stedman, 132.
6. Hays, 161.
7. Wiersbe, 102.
8. Timothy Keller, *Counterfeit Gods: The Empty Promises of Money, Sex, and Power, and the Only Hope That Matters* (New York: Dutton, 2009), xvii.
9. "Manna," *Old Testament Hebrew Lexicon,* http://www.biblestudytools.com/lexicons /hebrew/kjv/man.html.
10. Barclay, 106.
11. The commentaries and other sources our pilot group used to study 1 Corinthians 11:1-16 include the following (full citations are included in these Notes):
    The First Epistle to the Corinthians, C. K. Barrett.
    The NIV Application Commentary: 1 Corinthians, Craig L. Blomberg.
    The New Daily Study Bible: The Letters to the Corinthians, William Barclay.
    The First Epistle of Paul to the Corinthians, Charles R. Erdman.
    The First Epistle to the Corinthians, Gordon D. Fee.
    The Expositor's Bible Commentary, Frank E. Gaebelein.
    Interpretation: A Bible Commentary for Teaching and Preaching, First Corinthians, Richard B. Hays.
    The MacArthur New Testament Commentary: 1 Corinthians, John MacArthur.
    Letters to a Troubled Church, Ray C. Stedman.
    Be Wise, Warren W. Wiersbe.
    Paul for Everyone: 1 Corinthians, N. T. Wright.

12. Richard A. Horsley, *Abingdon New Testament Commentaries: 1 Corinthians* (Nashville: Abingdon Press, 1998), 153.
13. Erdman, 109.
14. "Sunetheia," *The KJV New Testament Greek Lexicon*, http://www.biblestudytools.com/lexicons/greek/kjv/sunetheia.html.
15. "Epitage," *The KJV New Testament Greek Lexicon*, http://www.biblestudytools.com/lexicons/greek/kjv/epitage.html.
16. Gaebelein, 255-256.
17. "Why do Jewish men wear yarmulkes (beanies) to cover their heads?" http://joi.org/qa/yarmulkas.shtml.
18. Gaebelein, 259.

Week 5
1. Wiersbe, 143.
2. "How Is Love Spelled Out in the Bible?" Richard J. Krejcir, *Discipleship Tools*, http://www.intothyword.org/apps/articles/default.asp?articleid=35437.
3. Barclay, 138.
4. Ibid., 144.
5. Ibid., 142.
6. Ibid., 147.
7. MacArthur, 371.
8. "Glossolalia," Encyclopedia Britannica, http://www.britannica.com/topic/glossolalia.
9. Hays, 235.
10. Blomberg, 273.
11. Hays, 238-239.
12. D. A. Carson, *Showing the Spirit: A Theological Exposition of 1 Corinthians 12–14* (Grand Rapids: Baker, 2000), 106.
13. MacArthur, 385.
14. Wiersbe,151.

Week 6
1. Barclay, 161.
2. Hays, 278.
3. Blomberg, 295.
4. Barclay, 166.
5. Early Church History – CH101, "CH101 - First Century Church History, The Primitive Church – 30-100 A.D.," http://www.churchhistory101.com/century1.php.
6. Hays, 259.
7. Barclay, 177.
8. Wiersbe, 169.
9. Philip Yancey, *Rumors of Another World: What on Earth Are We Missing?* (Grand Rapids: Zondervan, 2003), 201.
10. Wiersbe, 170.
11. Ibid., 169.
12. Stedman, 252.
13. C. S. Lewis, *Mere Christianity* (New York: Harper Collins, 1980) 86.
14. "Pulpit Commentary," 1 Corinthians 16:22, http://biblehub.com/1_corinthians/16-22.htm.

More from Melissa Spoelstra

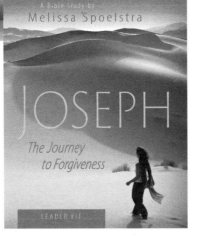

Jeremiah

Combining rich study of the Book of Jeremiah with practical life application for today, this study inspires us to dare to hope, remembering that God is rich in mercy and love.

978-1-4267-8897-0 (Leader Kit*)

Each leader kit includes a workbook, leader guide, and DVD (individual components also available separately).

Joseph

Explore what God has to say to us about grace and forgiveness through Joseph's story of trial and triumph found in Genesis 37-50. Learn from Joseph how to release your past and present hurts to God and allow Him to do a supernatural work of forgiveness in your life.

978-1-4267-8914-4 (Leader Kit*)

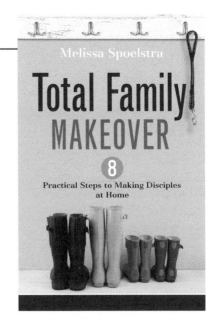

Total Family Makeover

This book gives you a spiritual track to run when it comes to making disciples at home, providing help for modeling and training your children in eight key areas. You'll love this practical approach to teaching children of all ages how to be followers of Jesus!

978-1-5018-2065-6